FRANKFURT TRAVEL GUIDE

The Ultimate Guide to Unveiling Frankfurt Ancient History, Art, Culture, Culinary Delights, and Breathtaking outdoor Activities

Spencer Reynolds

0

WELCOME 5

UNDERSTAND..13

   FRANKFURT PEOPLE..................................18

   THE HISTORY 22

   CULTURAL...30

   HERITAGE 38

   ART AND ARCHITECTURE 43

   FRANKFURT KITCHEN 48

   FRANKFURT NATIONAL PARK AND WILD LIFE.........56

SURVIVAL GUIDE **65**

   SUMMER 65

   WINTER 73

   SPRING 81

   ACCOMMODATION 86

   ELECTRICITY...91

   HEALTH 95

   INTERNET ACTIVITIES 99

   INTERNET CAFÉ 104

   MONEY AND CURRENCY EXCHANGE.....................109

   PUBLIC HOLIDAY 113

   WORK AND MINIMUM WAGE 118

   CUSTOMS AND REGULATIONS................125

ADVENTURES AND OUTDOORS ACTIVITIES...**131**

   TAUNUS MOUNTAINS..............................131

RHEIN RIVER 135

FRANKFURT GREEN BELT 139

OPEL ZOO 144

OUTDOOR SPORTS 147

GOETHE FOREST 151

OUTDOOR FESTIVALS AND EVENTS 155

HOT AIR BALLOON RIDES 159

THE FINEST RESTAURANTS, CLUBS, AND NIGHTTIME DELIGHTS 165

FINEST RESTAURANTS 165

TRENDY CLUBS 166

NIGHTTIME DELIGHTS 167

FRANKFURT ITINERARIES UNVEILING THE BEST OF FRANKFURT 171

7 DAYS ITINERARIES UNVEILING THE BEST OF FRANKFURT 171

TRANSPORTATION IN FRANKFURT NAVIGATING THE SCENIC ROUTES 179

PUBLIC TRANSPORTATION 179

REGIONAL TRAINS 180

CYCLING 181

SCENIC ROUTES AND DAY TRIPS 181

TAXIS AND RIDE-SHARING 182

PARKING 183

TICKETING AND FARES 183

LANGUAGE 185

CULTURAL CONSIDERATIONS 187

GREETINGS AND BASIC PHRASES 188

ENGAGING IN CONVERSATION 191

ORDERING FOOD AND DRINKS............................195

EXPLORING THE MARKETS 199

GETTING AROUND 203

TRADITIONAL FRANKFURT SAYINGS AND PROVERBS
....207

FRANKFURT LITERATURE AND POETRY 211

CULTURAL ETIQUETTE 214

LANGUAGE LEARNING RESOURCES 218

CONCLUSION 223

WELCOME

I sat at my desk, staring at my computer screen, feeling a mix of frustration and longing. It had been months since i last took a vacation, and the stress of my job had started to take a toll on me. I needed a getaway—a place where i could escape the demands of my daily routine and reconnect with myself.

As i scrolled through countless travel websites, my eyes suddenly landed on a mesmerizing image of Frankfurt. The vibrant cityscape, with its towering skyscrapers and historic landmarks, instantly captured my imagination. Intrigued, i began to dig deeper, uncovering the city's rich history and diverse culture.

Something about Frankfurt tugged at my heartstrings. I felt an inexplicable connection to a place i had never been before. The more i read about its ancient past and modern present, the more i realized that this was the perfect destination for my much-needed vacation.

Frankfurt seemed to offer the best of both worlds—a captivating blend of ancient history and contemporary allure. It was a city where the past and present intertwined, creating a unique atmosphere that beckoned me to explore. The thought of wandering through cobblestone streets, discovering hidden corners of the Old Town, and standing in awe of the majestic Römer filled me with excitement.

But it wasn't just the history that drew me to Frankfurt. It was the promise of a cultural feast that awaited me. The city boasted an impressive array of museums and galleries, showcasing a diverse range of artistic expressions. I imagined myself immersing in the works of renowned masters and being inspired by the innovative creations of contemporary artists.

The allure of Frankfurt's culinary delights also played a significant role in my decision. I had always been a food enthusiast, and the thought of indulging in traditional Apfelwein, savoring mouthwatering German sausages, and exploring the city's vibrant food markets made my taste buds tingle with anticipation. The city's reputation as a culinary hub, with its blend of local and international flavors, promised an unforgettable gastronomic adventure.

But above all, it was the emotional connection that i felt with Frankfurt that sealed the deal. I yearned for a destination that would evoke a sense of wonder and rejuvenate my spirit. Frankfurt, with its ancient history, thriving art scene, and breathtaking outdoor spaces, seemed to hold the key to my soul's desire for exploration and renewal.

With a newfound determination, i booked my flight to Frankfurt, feeling a mixture of excitement and contentment. I knew that this journey would be more than just a vacation— it would be a transformative experience. In the embrace of Frankfurt's enchanting streets and vibrant culture, i was ready to rediscover myself, to open my heart to new possibilities, and to create lasting memories that would forever be etched in my soul.

Welcome to the enchanting city of Frankfurt, where ancient history meets vibrant modernity in a mesmerizing blend of art, culture, and culinary delights. As you flip through the pages of this comprehensive travel guide, get ready to embark on an unforgettable journey through the heart of Germany. Discover the hidden treasures of a city steeped in rich heritage, where towering skyscrapers share the skyline with historic landmarks, and cobblestone streets lead you to a world of captivating experiences.

Frankfurt, a city of contrasts, invites you to delve into its ancient history that dates back over a thousand years. Uncover the secrets of the Old Town, where magnificent medieval buildings whisper tales of emperors and knights. Stroll along the banks of the serene Main River, tracing the footsteps of ancient traders and exploring the birthplace of the European banking system. Immerse yourself in the timeless beauty of the Römer, the iconic town hall, and lose yourself in the intricate details of the stunning Frankfurt Cathedral.

But Frankfurt is not just a city frozen in time; it is a dynamic metropolis that pulsates with contemporary energy. Marvel at the modern marvels of the Frankfurt skyline, adorned with futuristic skyscrapers that have earned it the nickname "Mainhattan." Lose yourself in the city's thriving arts scene, where world-class museums and galleries showcase everything from classical masterpieces to avant-garde installations. Indulge your taste buds in the culinary delights of Frankfurt, where traditional Apfelwein taverns sit alongside Michelin-starred restaurants, offering a delectable blend of local and international flavors.

For those seeking outdoor adventures, Frankfurt has an abundance of natural beauty to offer. Explore the lush green spaces of Palmengarten and Grüneburgpark, where blooming flowers and tranquil ponds create an oasis of serenity within the bustling city.

Take a leisurely boat ride along the Main River, absorbing the breathtaking views of the surrounding landscapes. And if you're feeling Adventurous, venture beyond the city limits to discover the stunning Taunus Mountains, where hiking trails and picturesque villages await your exploration.

Whether you're a history buff, an art enthusiast, a food lover, or an outdoor adventurer, Frankfurt has something extraordinary to offer you. In this ultimate travel guide, we have curated the best of the city's ancient history, art, culture, culinary delights, and breathtaking outdoor activities, providing you with a roadmap to an unforgettable Frankfurt experience. So pack your bags, open your mind, and get ready to uncover the secrets of Frankfurt, where tradition and innovation intertwine to create a city like no other.

UNDERSTAND

In order to truly appreciate and connect with the city of Frankfurt, it is essential to delve into its essence and understand the various aspects that make it a unique and captivating destination. From its history to its culture, from its people to its traditions, gaining a deeper understanding of Frankfurt allows visitors to forge a meaningful connection with this vibrant city.

Historical Significance

To understand Frankfurt, one must explore its rich historical heritage. The city's roots can be traced back to ancient times, with evidence of settlements dating as far back as the Roman era. Frankfurt played a pivotal role in the Holy Roman Empire, serving as the coronation site of emperors and an important trading hub. The impact of World War II is also a significant part of Frankfurt's history, as the city underwent extensive reconstruction, transforming into a modern metropolis.

Architectural Marvels

Frankfurt's architectural landscape reflects its diverse history. Exploring the city's streets reveals a captivating blend of ancient and modern structures. The Römer, a symbol of the city's medieval past, stands proudly in the historic heart of Frankfurt; while nearby, towering skyscrapers dominate the skyline, earning the city the moniker "Mainhattan." Understanding Frankfurt means appreciating the harmonious coexistence of centuries-old buildings and cutting-edge architectural marvels.

Cultural Fusion

Frankfurt is a melting pot of cultures, traditions, and influences. The city's multicultural fabric is evident in its vibrant neighborhoods, each with its own distinct character. From the trendy Sachsenhausen district to the bohemian vibes of Bornheim, Frankfurt's diverse communities contribute to its cosmopolitan allure. Exploring these neighborhoods, mingling with locals, sampling their cuisines offers an opportunity to truly grasp the cultural tapestry that defines the city.

Museums and Art Galleries

Frankfurt's love for art and culture is evident in its numerous museums and art galleries. The Museumsufer, or Museum Embankment, boasts an impressive collection of museums, including the Städel Museum, showcasing European art from the middle Ages to the present, and the Museum of Modern Art (MMK), featuring contemporary works. Understanding Frankfurt's artistic side involves immersing oneself in these cultural institutions, appreciating the masterpieces they hold, and embracing the city's creative spirit.

Festivals and Traditions

Participating in Frankfurt's festivals and traditions provides a deeper understanding of the city's local customs and way of life. From the lively atmosphere of the Frankfurt Christmas Market to the exuberant celebration of the Museum Embankment Festival, these events offer a glimpse into the city's traditions, gastronomy, and convivial spirit. Embracing Frankfurt's festive side allows visitors to connect with the city's vibrant energy and appreciate the joyous moments that bring its communities together.

Green Spaces and Outdoor Activities

Frankfurt's commitment to preserving green spaces amidst its urban landscape is another facet that must be understood. The city boasts beautiful parks, such as the Palmengarten and the expansive Grüneburgpark, offering tranquil retreats for relaxation and recreation. Exploring the banks of the Main River, cycling along its scenic paths, or even embarking on a boat tour provides an opportunity to understand Frankfurt's harmonious coexistence with nature.

By seeking to understand Frankfurt beyond its surface, visitors can immerse themselves in the city's history, architecture, culture, and traditions. This deeper understanding fosters a genuine connection, allowing travelers to appreciate the city's multifaceted charm and create lasting memories that go beyond mere sightseeing. Frankfurt, with its layers of complexity and captivating spirit, invites visitors to explore, learn, and embrace the heart and soul of the city.

Frankfurt people

The people of Frankfurt are an integral part of the city's vibrant tapestry, contributing to its dynamic atmosphere and diverse cultural landscape. Understanding the people of Frankfurt is essential to truly grasp the city's spirit and forge meaningful connections during your visit. Here are some key aspects to consider:

Warm Hospitality

Frankfurters are known for their warm and welcoming nature. Visitors to the city often encounter friendly faces ready to assist and engage in conversation. Whether it's asking for directions, seeking recommendations, or simply striking up a conversation in a café, locals are generally open, approachable, and eager to share their love for their city.

Multicultural Fusion

Frankfurt is a multicultural hub, with people from various backgrounds and nationalities calling it home. This cultural fusion is reflected in the city's diverse neighborhoods, international cuisine, and a rich tapestry of traditions. The openness and acceptance of different cultures contribute to Frankfurt's cosmopolitan atmosphere, creating a sense of unity within its diversity.

Work Ethic

Frankfurters have a reputation for their strong work ethic and drive. As a financial and business center, the city is home to numerous professionals dedicated to their careers. This industrious spirit permeates various aspects of life in Frankfurt, fostering an environment of innovation, efficiency, and ambition.

Pride in Heritage

Despite being a modern metropolis, Frankfurters take pride in their city's rich history and heritage. The deep-rooted connection to Frankfurt's past is evident in the preservation of historical landmarks, the celebration of local traditions, and the respect for cultural legacies. Locals often display a sense of pride when sharing stories about their city's past, further enhancing visitors' understanding and appreciation of Frankfurt's heritage.

Cultural Engagement

Frankfurt's residents actively engage in cultural activities, contributing to the city's thriving arts and entertainment scene. The locals take advantage of the numerous museums, theaters, and galleries, demonstrating a genuine appreciation for artistic expression. Visitors can witness this enthusiasm by attending cultural events, performances, or simply observing the city's vibrant street art and creative initiatives.

Love for Culinary Delights

Food plays a significant role in the lives of Frankfurters, and their culinary traditions are cherished. From traditional Apfelwein taverns serving regional specialties to international restaurants offering global cuisines, Frankfurt's gastronomic scene is a reflection of its cosmopolitan nature. Sharing a meal and experiencing the local delicacies provides an opportunity to connect with the people of Frankfurt, fostering a deeper understanding of their cultural identity.

Understanding the people of Frankfurt means embracing their warmth, multiculturalism work ethic, and pride in heritage, cultural engagement, and love for food. Interacting with locals, striking up conversations, and immersing oneself in the city's vibrant atmosphere allow visitors to forge meaningful connections, gain insights into local life, and create lasting memories of their Frankfurt experience.

The History

The history of Frankfurt is a captivating journey that spans over a thousand years, marked by significant events and cultural transformations. From its humble beginnings as a small medieval settlement to its current status as a global financial hub, Frankfurt's historical narrative is woven into the fabric of its streets and landmarks. Let's explore the key chapters of Frankfurt's history:

Early Settlement and Imperial City

Frankfurt's history dates back to the Roman era when a small settlement named "Nida" was established along the banks of the Main River. This strategic location offered access to trade routes and fertile lands, attracting settlers. However, it was during the early middle Ages that Frankfurt truly began to flourish. In the 9th century, it gained prominence as an imperial city within the Holy Roman Empire. The city was granted various privileges and rights by Holy Roman Emperors, allowing it to govern itself independently and prosper as a political and cultural center.

The Coronations at Frankfurt's Cathedral

Frankfurt's significance as an imperial city was further solidified by the tradition of coronations that took place at the city's Cathedral. Starting in the 13th century, emperors from the Holy Roman Empire were crowned in Frankfurt, cementing the city's role as a focal point of imperial power. These coronations attracted nobility, dignitaries, and travelers from across Europe, contributing to the city's prestige and economic growth.

Trade and Commerce

Frankfurt's favorable location along the Main River and its position as a crossroads between northern and southern Europe made it an ideal trading hub. The city's annual trade fairs, starting in the 12th century, played a crucial role in its economic development. These fairs attracted merchants, artisans, and traders from far and wide, fostering a vibrant marketplace where goods, ideas, and cultures intermingled. Frankfurt's participation in the Hanseatic League during the 16th century further enhanced its commercial influence, enabling it to engage in lucrative trade partnerships and solidify its status as a prosperous city.

The Gutenberg Revolution

One of Frankfurt's most significant contributions to human history came in the form of the printing revolution. In the 15th century, Johannes Gutenberg, a native of the city, developed the revolutionary printing press with movable type. This groundbreaking invention transformed the way information was disseminated, allowing for the mass production of books and facilitating the spread of knowledge across Europe. Gutenberg's printing press laid the foundation for Frankfurt to become a prominent center for printing and publishing, with numerous printing houses and publishing firms emerging in the city.

Modernization and World War II

During the 19th century, Frankfurt underwent a period of modernization and urban development. The construction of a comprehensive railway network and the establishment of the Main River embankment were instrumental in facilitating transportation and connecting Frankfurt to the broader region. The city embraced industrialization and experienced rapid growth, with new residential and commercial districts emerging.

However, Frankfurt's progress was halted by the devastating impact of World War II. The city suffered extensive damage due to bombings, resulting in the destruction of many historical buildings and landmarks. The post-war reconstruction efforts aimed to restore Frankfurt's former glory while incorporating modern architectural styles. Today, the city's skyline showcases a juxtaposition of old and new, with historic buildings standing alongside contemporary skyscrapers.

Financial and Business Hub

In the post-war era, Frankfurt embarked on a remarkable transformation, establishing itself as a global financial and business hub. In 1948, the Deutsche Bundesbank, Germany's central bank, was founded in Frankfurt, solidifying its position as a financial center. The Frankfurt Stock Exchange also rose to prominence, attracting international investors and becoming one of the largest stock exchanges in the world. The concentration of banks, financial institutions, and multinational corporations in Frankfurt earned it the nickname "Bankfurt" and further bolstered its status as a leading financial destination in Europe.

Cultural and Artistic Heritage

Frankfurt's rich cultural heritage is exemplified through its diverse range of museums, galleries, and cultural institutions. The Städel Museum, founded in 1815, houses an extensive collection of European art, spanning from the middle Ages to the present day. It showcases masterpieces by renowned artists such as Rembrandt, Monet, Picasso, and many others, offering visitors a journey through the history of European art. The Museum of Modern Art (MMK) is another gem in Frankfurt's cultural landscape, dedicated to contemporary art and innovative artistic expressions.

In addition to its impressive art museums, Frankfurt is home to a vibrant theater scene. The Frankfurt Opera, with its stunning architecture, hosts world-class opera performances, ballets, and classical concerts. The Schauspiel Frankfurt, a renowned theater company, presents a diverse repertoire of plays and performances, ranging from classic works to contemporary productions. The city also hosts a variety of festivals and cultural events throughout the year, including the Frankfurt Book Fair, one of the largest book fairs in the world, attracting publishers, authors, and book enthusiasts from every corner of the globe.

Frankfurt's cultural heritage is not limited to the arts alone. The city takes great pride in preserving its historical landmarks, such as the Römer, a medieval town hall with its iconic stepped gables, and the Kaiserdom, Frankfurt's Cathedral, which showcases stunning Gothic architecture. These architectural treasures serve as tangible links to Frankfurt's past, inviting visitors to step back in time and experience the city's rich history firsthand.

Moreover, Frankfurt's cultural diversity is celebrated through its vibrant neighborhoods and multicultural events. The Bahnhofsviertel, situated near the central train station, is a melting pot of different cultures, with a lively atmosphere filled with international restaurants, trendy bars, and a vibrant nightlife scene. The district of Sachsenhausen is known for its traditional Apfelwein taverns, where locals and visitors gather to enjoy the local apple wine and hearty German cuisine.

As you explore Frankfurt's cultural heritage, you'll also notice the city's commitment to contemporary architecture and urban design. The skyline of Frankfurt, dominated by towering skyscrapers, is a testament to the city's modern identity and its status as a leading financial center. The Main Tower, with its observation deck offering panoramic views of the city, provides a unique perspective on the blend of historic and modern architecture that defines Frankfurt's cityscape.

In conclusion, Frankfurt's cultural and artistic heritage is a tapestry woven with layers of history, creativity, and diversity. From its early days as an imperial city to its current status as a global financial powerhouse, Frankfurt has continuously evolved while embracing its past. Exploring the city's museums, theaters, historical landmarks, and vibrant neighborhoods allows visitors to immerse themselves in the rich cultural fabric of Frankfurt, creating lasting memories and a deeper appreciation for its remarkable heritage.

Cultural

The cultural scene in Frankfurt is vibrant, diverse, and brimming with artistic expressions from various disciplines. From world-class museums and galleries to lively music and theater performances, Frankfurt offers a wealth of cultural experiences. Let's delve into the cultural aspects that make Frankfurt a captivating destination:

Museums and Art Galleries

Frankfurt is home to an impressive array of museums and art galleries, showcasing a vast range of artistic styles and historical artifacts. The Städel Museum stands as a crown jewel of the city's cultural landscape, housing an extensive collection of European art spanning from the middle Ages to contemporary works. It features masterpieces by renowned artists such as Botticelli, Rembrandt, Van Gogh, and Picasso. The Museum of Modern Art (MMK) is dedicated to contemporary art, featuring thought-provoking exhibitions and installations by both established and emerging artists.

Music and Theater

Frankfurt boasts a rich music and theater scene that caters to diverse tastes. The Frankfurt Opera is internationally acclaimed for its world-class opera performances, ballets, and classical concerts. The opera house itself is a magnificent architectural masterpiece. The Alte Oper (Old Opera House) hosts a variety of concerts, including classical, jazz, and contemporary music. For theater enthusiasts, the Schauspiel Frankfurt presents an exciting repertoire of plays, ranging from classic works to avant-garde productions. The English Theatre Frankfurt offers English-language productions, catering to the city's international community.

Festivals and Cultural Events

Frankfurt comes alive with a calendar full of festivals and cultural events throughout the year. The Frankfurt Book Fair is a highlight, attracting publishers, authors, and literary enthusiasts from around the world. It is an essential platform for the publishing industry and a hub of literary exchange. The Museumsuferfest, held along the banks of the Main River, is a vibrant cultural festival featuring music, dance, art, and culinary delights from different cultures. The Mainova Frankfurt Marathon is another significant event, drawing runners and spectators to the city's streets in a celebration of athleticism and community spirit.

Culinary Delights

Frankfurt's cultural scene extends to its culinary offerings, with a diverse range of gastronomic experiences to indulge in. The city is renowned for its Apfelwein (apple wine) and traditional Apfelwein taverns, where locals and visitors gather to enjoy this regional specialty along with hearty German cuisine. Sachsenhausen, a district famous for its Apfelwein taverns, provides an authentic experience in a lively atmosphere. The Kleinmarkthalle, a bustling indoor market, offers a sensory feast of fresh produce, gourmet delicacies, and international flavors.

Multicultural Neighborhoods

Frankfurt's cultural fabric is enriched by its multicultural neighborhoods. The Bahnhofsviertel, located near the central train station, is a melting pot of different cultures and cuisines, reflecting the city's cosmopolitan nature. This dynamic district is filled with international restaurants, vibrant bars, and a thriving nightlife scene. Another multicultural gem is the district of Bornheim, known for its charming streets lined with international eateries, cafes, and boutiques.

Cultural Heritage and Architecture

Frankfurt proudly preserves its cultural heritage through its historical landmarks and architectural treasures. The Römer, Frankfurt's medieval town hall, is an iconic symbol of the city. Its charming stepped gables and inner courtyards transport visitors back in time. The Kaiserdom, Frankfurt's

Cathedral, is a majestic Gothic structure that holds centuries of history within its walls. The Palmengarten, a botanical garden, offers a serene escape and showcases a vast array of plant species from around the world.

In conclusion, Frankfurt's cultural scene is a tapestry of artistic expressions, historical richness, and diverse influences. The city's museums, music and theater performances, festivals, culinary experiences, multicultural neighborhoods, and architectural landmarks all contribute to the cultural tapestry of Frankfurt. Whether you're a lover of art, music, literature, or gastronomy, Frankfurt offers a myriad of opportunities to immerse yourself in its vibrant cultural offerings.

Beyond the traditional art forms, Frankfurt embraces contemporary cultural expressions as well. The city nurtures a thriving contemporary art scene with numerous galleries and exhibition spaces that showcase the works of local and international artists pushing boundaries and exploring new artistic frontiers. The Dialogmuseum provides a unique sensory experience, inviting visitors to explore the world in complete darkness, fostering empathy and understanding for the visually impaired.

Frankfurt's commitment to cultural diversity is evident in its ongoing efforts to promote inclusivity and intercultural dialogue. The city hosts events that celebrate different ethnicities, traditions, and perspectives, fostering a sense of unity and mutual respect. The Dippemess, a traditional folk festival, brings together people from all walks of life to enjoy rides, games, and local delicacies, creating a lively atmosphere of communal celebration.

Frankfurt's cultural scene is also deeply intertwined with its academic institutions and intellectual pursuits. The city is home to esteemed universities and research centers that foster intellectual curiosity and academic excellence. Lectures, seminars, and public discussions on a wide range of topics are regularly organized, inviting locals and visitors alike to engage in intellectual discourse and expand their knowledge.

Furthermore, Frankfurt's cultural richness extends beyond its borders. As a truly international city, it embraces global influences and hosts international film festivals, music concerts, and performing arts events that showcase the talents of artists from around the world. This global outlook is also reflected in the city's thriving international community, which contributes to the diversity and multicultural fabric of Frankfurt's cultural landscape.

In summary, Frankfurt's cultural scene is a mosaic of historical heritage, artistic expressions, contemporary creativity, and multicultural influences. The city's museums, theaters, festivals, culinary experiences, and multicultural neighborhoods provide a vibrant tapestry of cultural encounters for visitors to explore and enjoy. Whether you're strolling through art galleries, attending a world-class opera performance, indulging in diverse culinary delights, or participating in multicultural celebrations, Frankfurt promises an enriching and immersive cultural experience for all.

Heritage

Frankfurt's heritage is a testament to its rich history and cultural significance. The city's architectural landmarks, historical sites, and preservation efforts combine to create a captivating tapestry of heritage that tells the story of Frankfurt's past. Let's explore some of the key aspects of Frankfurt's heritage:

Architectural Landmarks

Frankfurt's skyline showcases a captivating blend of architectural styles spanning centuries. The Römer, Frankfurt's medieval town hall, stands as an iconic symbol of the city. With its distinctive stepped gables and intricate facade, the Römer has been a focal point of Frankfurt's political and social life for centuries. Adjacent to the Römer, the Römerberg square is a charming ensemble of half-timbered houses, showcasing the city's medieval architectural heritage.

Another architectural gem is the Kaiserdom, Frankfurt's Cathedral. This imposing Gothic structure is a testament to the city's historical and religious significance. The cathedral's stunning interiors, intricate stained glass windows, and towering spires inspire awe and offer a glimpse into Frankfurt's spiritual heritage.

Historical Sites

Frankfurt is steeped in history, and numerous historical sites bear witness to its past. The Paulskirche, also known as St. Paul's Church, holds great historical significance as the birthplace of German democracy. It was here, in 1848, that the first freely elected German National Assembly convened, marking an important milestone in Germany's political history.

The Goethe House and Museum provide insight into the life and works of Johann Wolfgang von Goethe, one of Germany's most celebrated literary figures. The house, where Goethe was born and raised, has been meticulously preserved, allowing visitors to immerse themselves in the world of this influential writer.

Preservation and Restoration

Frankfurt places great importance on the preservation and restoration of its heritage. The reconstruction of historical buildings damaged during World War II has been a significant undertaking. The Old Town (Altstadt) restoration project, initiated in the 1980s, aimed to recreate the medieval charm and architectural character of the area. Today, visitors can explore the reconstructed Altstadt, with its narrow cobblestone streets, charming squares, and meticulously restored buildings.

The preservation efforts extend beyond individual structures. Frankfurt's commitment to preserving its heritage is evident in the ongoing maintenance and restoration of its architectural ensembles, public spaces, and historical landmarks. These efforts ensure that Frankfurt's heritage remains vibrant and accessible to both residents and visitors.

Museums and Cultural Institutions

Frankfurt's museums and cultural institutions play a vital role in preserving and showcasing the city's heritage. The Historical Museum Frankfurt offers a comprehensive overview of Frankfurt's history, displaying artifacts, documents, and multimedia presentations that provide insights into the city's evolution over time. The Museum Judengasse explores Frankfurt's Jewish history and culture, highlighting the significance of the Jewish community in the city.

The Archaeological Museum Frankfurt sheds light on the ancient history of the region, with exhibits ranging from prehistoric artifacts to Roman antiquities. These museums, among others, serve as custodians of Frankfurt's heritage, offering visitors an immersive experience that deepens their understanding of the city's historical legacy.

In conclusion, Frankfurt's heritage is a tapestry woven with architectural marvels, historical landmarks, and preservation efforts that bring the city's past to life. From the iconic Römer and Kaiserdom to the meticulously restored Altstadt, Frankfurt's heritage invites exploration and offers a glimpse into its rich history. The city's museums and cultural institutions further contribute to preserving and presenting Frankfurt's heritage, ensuring that future generations can appreciate and learn from its legacy.

Art and Architecture

Frankfurt's art and architecture scene is a captivating blend of historical grandeur and contemporary creativity. The city's architectural diversity, ranging from medieval structures to modern skyscrapers, is complemented by a vibrant art scene that celebrates both traditional and innovative artistic expressions. Let's delve into the art and architecture of Frankfurt in more detail:

Architectural Marvels

Frankfurt's skyline is a striking fusion of architectural styles, representing different eras and influences. The Main Tower, one of the city's modern landmarks, offers panoramic views of Frankfurt and its surrounding areas. Its sleek design and glass façade make it a standout feature in the city's skyline.

Another notable architectural marvel is the Frankfurt Cathedral, also known as the Kaiserdom. This impressive Gothic structure dates back to the 14th century and features intricate stone carvings, stunning stained glass windows, and towering spires. Its grandeur and historical significance make it a must-visit landmark for architecture enthusiasts.

The Museum Embankment, or Museumsufer, is a picturesque area along the banks of the Main River that showcases a collection of remarkable museums housed in diverse architectural styles. From the classical elegance of the Städel Museum to the modernist design of the Museum of Applied Arts (Museum Angewandte Kunst), this riverside promenade is a treasure trove for art and architecture lovers.

Contemporary Architecture

As a global financial hub, Frankfurt is renowned for its modern architecture, particularly in the financial district known as the Bankenviertel. The Commerzbank Tower, with its distinctive wedge-shaped design, was once the tallest building in Europe and exemplifies Frankfurt's commitment to cutting-edge architecture.

The Messeturm (Trade Fair Tower) is another iconic skyscraper that graces the Frankfurt skyline. Its triangular shape and mirrored façade make it a standout feature, reflecting the city's ambition and modernity.

Museums and Galleries

Frankfurt is home to a wealth of museums and galleries that cater to diverse artistic tastes. The Städel Museum, one of Germany's most renowned art museums, boasts a vast collection spanning seven centuries of European art. It houses works by masters such as Rembrandt, Botticelli, Monet, and

Van Gogh, providing visitors with a comprehensive journey through art history.

The Museum of Modern Art (MMK) is a cutting-edge institution dedicated to contemporary art. Its striking architecture, characterized by cubic forms and expansive windows, perfectly complements the innovative artworks it showcases. The MMK Zollamt, an annex of the museum, is a former customs building that now serves as a platform for experimental and interdisciplinary contemporary art.

Street Art and Urban Creativity

Frankfurt embraces urban creativity, and its streets and neighborhoods serve as canvases for vibrant street art and graffiti. The Bahnhofsviertel, with its dynamic and multicultural atmosphere, is known for its street art scene. Walking through its streets reveals colorful murals and urban interventions that add an edgy and creative flair to the cityscape.

The Naxos-Halle, a former industrial site transformed into a cultural center, showcases the city's commitment to repurposing spaces for artistic endeavors. This multifunctional venue hosts exhibitions, performances, and events, fostering a dynamic and experimental artistic community.

In conclusion, Frankfurt's art and architecture scene seamlessly blends historical landmarks with contemporary creations. From the grandeur of the Frankfurt Cathedral and the Städel Museum to the modern skyscrapers of the financial district and the vibrant street art adorning its walls, Frankfurt offers a rich tapestry of artistic expressions. Whether you're captivated by centuries-old masterpieces or fascinated by avant-garde contemporary art, Frankfurt's art and architecture will inspire and delight at every turn.

Frankfurt kitchen

Frankfurt's culinary scene is a delightful fusion of traditional German cuisine, international flavors, and a burgeoning food culture. The city's kitchen offers a range of delectable dishes, from hearty regional specialties to innovative culinary creations. Let's explore the flavors and culinary experiences that wait in the kitchens of Frankfurt:

Traditional German Cuisine

Frankfurt is known for its traditional German dishes that exemplify the country's rich culinary heritage. One iconic Frankfurt specialty is the "Frankfurter Grüne Sauce" (Green Sauce), a cold herb sauce made from a blend of seven different herbs, including parsley, chives, and sorrel. This tangy and refreshing sauce is traditionally served with boiled eggs and potatoes, creating a harmonious combination of flavors.

Another beloved traditional dish is "Frankfurter Rippchen" (Frankfurt-style ribs). These succulent, slow-cooked pork ribs are typically marinated in savory brine, then roasted until tender. Served with sauerkraut and mustard, Frankfurter Rippchen is a delicious and satisfying meal that showcases the region's affinity for pork-based dishes.

Apfelwein and Regional Drinks

No culinary exploration of Frankfurt is complete without trying the local beverage known as "Apfelwein" or "Ebbelwoi." This tart and refreshing apple cider has deep roots in Frankfurt's culture and is traditionally served in ceramic mugs called "Bembel." Immerse yourself in the traditional Apfelwein taverns, known as "Ebbelwoi-Kneipen," where you can enjoy a glass of this iconic beverage while savoring regional dishes and lively atmosphere.

Beyond Apfelwein, Frankfurt boasts a thriving beer culture, with numerous breweries and beer gardens offering a variety of local and international brews. Sample Frankfurt's craft beers or indulge in classic German beer styles while enjoying the convivial atmosphere of a beer garden.

International Flavors

Frankfurt's diverse population and cosmopolitan nature have influenced its culinary landscape, offering a wide array of international cuisines. Explore the multicultural neighborhood of Bahnhofsviertel, where you can find a vibrant selection of Middle Eastern, Asian, and African eateries serving up flavors from around the world. From fragrant falafel wraps to aromatic curry dishes, Frankfurt's international culinary offerings cater to every palate.

Culinary Innovations

Frankfurt is also a city at the forefront of culinary innovation, with a growing number of innovative restaurants and food concepts.

Experience the creativity of Frankfurt's contemporary food scene, where chefs blend traditional techniques with modern twists and incorporate seasonal, locally sourced ingredients. From avant-garde tasting menus to fusion cuisine that combines diverse culinary traditions, Frankfurt's culinary innovators are redefining the city's gastronomic landscape.

Farmers Markets and Food Festivals

Immerse yourself in Frankfurt's culinary culture by exploring its vibrant farmers markets. The Kleinmarkthalle, located in the city center, offers a feast for the senses with its stalls brimming with fresh produce, local cheeses, meats, and artisanal products. Engage with local vendors, taste regional specialties, and discover the finest ingredients that contribute to Frankfurt's culinary excellence.

Throughout the year, Frankfurt hosts various food festivals and events that celebrate gastronomy. From the annual Apfelwein Festival to the Street Food Festival, these events showcase the city's culinary diversity and provide opportunities to indulge in a wide range of flavors and culinary experiences.

In conclusion, Frankfurt's kitchen is a delightful tapestry of traditional German cuisine, international flavors, culinary innovations, and vibrant food culture. Whether you're savoring a classic dish like Frankfurter Grüne Sauce, exploring international flavors in multicultural neighborhoods, or indulging in culinary creations from visionary chefs,

Frankfurt offers a culinary journey that caters to every taste and preference. The city's kitchens are a testament to its vibrant and evolving food scene, where tradition and innovation seamlessly blend to create memorable dining experiences.

Gourmet Dining

For those seeking a refined culinary experience, Frankfurt is home to a number of Michelin-starred restaurants and fine dining establishments. These venues showcase the skills of talented chefs who masterfully create artful dishes using the finest ingredients. Immerse yourself in a world of gastronomic excellence as you indulge in meticulously crafted tasting menus, expertly paired wines, and impeccable service.

Street Food and Markets

Frankfurt's street food scene is thriving, offering a tantalizing array of flavors from around the globe. Food trucks and stalls can be found at various locations throughout the city, serving up mouthwatering delights such as gourmet burgers, exotic wraps, artisanal ice cream, and much more. Explore the vibrant food markets like the Markthalle Höchst or the Wochenmarkt Konstablerwache, where you can sample a diverse range of local and international culinary creations.

Baking and Confectionery

Frankfurt has a rich tradition of baking and confectionery, with a plethora of bakeries and pastry shops that tempt passersby with their delectable treats. Indulge in freshly baked bread, traditional pastries like the Bethmännchen (marzipan cookies), or the famous Frankfurter Kranz, a rich buttercream-filled cake coated with nuts and cherries. These sweet delights are the perfect accompaniment to a cup of coffee as you relax and soak in the city's ambiance.

Culinary Events and Workshops

For those interested in learning more about Frankfurt's culinary traditions, attending culinary events and workshops can be a fantastic way to immerse you in the city's food culture. From cooking classes that teach you how to prepare traditional dishes to wine tastings that showcase the region's best vintages, this experience provide insight into the ingredients, techniques, and flavors that define Frankfurt's kitchen.

Culinary Souvenirs

Don't forget to bring a piece of Frankfurt's kitchen back home with you. Visit specialty food shops and delicatessens to discover an array of local products, including regional cheeses, cured meats, mustard, and jams. You can also find unique kitchenware and culinary gadgets that make for excellent souvenirs, allowing you to recreate a taste of Frankfurt in your own home.

In conclusion, Frankfurt's kitchen is a captivating tapestry of flavors, traditions, and innovations. From savoring traditional German dishes to exploring international cuisines, indulging in gourmet dining to immersing yourself in street food delights, Frankfurt offers a culinary experience that is diverse, enticing, and unforgettable. So, prepare your taste buds for a culinary adventure as you explore the kitchens of

Frankfurt and discover the city's gastronomic treasures.

Frankfurt National Park and Wild Life

Frankfurt is surrounded by natural beauty, and within its proximity lays a haven for nature enthusiasts and wildlife lovers. The region boasts several national parks, protected areas, and nature reserves that offer opportunities to immerse you in breathtaking landscapes and encounter diverse wildlife. Let's explore the national parks and wildlife of Frankfurt in more detail:

Odenwald Nature Park

Located on the northeastern edge of Frankfurt, the Odenwald Nature Park is a sprawling expanse of forested hills, winding rivers, and picturesque valleys. This protected area is renowned for its natural beauty and diverse wildlife. Explore the network of hiking trails that meander through ancient woodlands, discover hidden waterfalls, and marvel at the panoramic views from elevated viewpoints. The Odenwald Nature Park is home to various species of birds, including the majestic red kite and the elusive black stork. Keep an eye out for deer, wild boar, and foxes that roam freely in this enchanting wilderness.

Taunus Nature Park

To the north of Frankfurt lies the Taunus Nature Park, a vast region of rolling hills, dense forests, and charming villages. This protected area offers countless opportunities for outdoor activities and wildlife observation. Hike along scenic trails that lead to panoramic viewpoints, explore pristine rivers and lakes, or embark on a cycling adventure through the picturesque countryside. The Taunus Nature Park is home to a rich variety of wildlife, including the European wildcat, the red deer, and numerous bird species. Nature enthusiasts will also appreciate the abundance of wildflowers, rare orchids, and lush vegetation that adorn the park's landscapes.

Vogelsberg Nature Park

Located northeast of Frankfurt, the Vogelsberg Nature Park is characterized by its volcanic peaks, sprawling meadows, and dense forests. This scenic region is a paradise for hikers, offering an extensive network of trails that wind through volcanic landscapes and lead to breathtaking viewpoints. The Vogelsberg Nature Park is home to a diverse range of fauna, including golden eagles, peregrine falcons, and wildcats. Explore the park's picturesque lakes and rivers, go fishing, or simply immerse yourself in the tranquility of nature.

Wildlife Conservation Centers

Frankfurt is also home to several wildlife conservation centers and zoological parks that aim to protect and preserve endangered species. The Opel Zoo, located just outside of

Frankfurt, is a popular destination for families and nature enthusiasts. This expansive zoo is known for its efforts in wildlife conservation and houses a wide variety of animals, including big cats, primates, and rare bird species. Visitors can learn about conservation initiatives and observe animals in naturalistic habitats.

Birdwatching and Nature Observatories

Nature enthusiasts will find Frankfurt to be a paradise for birdwatching. Along the Main River, you can find several nature observatories and bird hides where you can observe native and migratory bird species. These designated areas provide a peaceful environment for birdwatchers to spot herons, kingfishers, and other avian species that inhabit the riverbanks and wetlands.

In conclusion, Frankfurt's surrounding region offers a wealth of natural treasures, from expansive national parks to protected areas teeming with wildlife. Whether you're hiking through ancient forests, observing rare bird species, or simply immersing yourself in the beauty of pristine landscapes, Frankfurt's national parks and wildlife provide a serene escape from urban life. So, embark on an adventure and discover the diverse ecosystems and fascinating wildlife that thrive in the natural havens around Frankfurt.

Rhine-Main Biosphere Reserve

The Rhine-Main Biosphere Reserve, located in the vicinity of Frankfurt, is a unique and ecologically diverse area that encompasses wetlands, floodplains, forests, and meadows. This UNESCO-designated reserve serves as a vital habitat for numerous plant and animal species. Explore the network of trails that wind through the reserve, allowing you to observe the rich biodiversity up close. Look out for rare bird species, such as the great egret and the black stork, as well as amphibians, reptiles, and a variety of insect species. The Rhine-Main Biosphere Reserve also plays a crucial role in protecting and restoring valuable ecosystems and promoting sustainable land management practices.

Nidda Nature Reserve

Stretching along the Nidda River, the Nidda Nature Reserve is a picturesque area that offers a peaceful retreat from the bustling city. This protected reserve is characterized by its meandering river, meadows, and floodplain forests. Explore the network of walking and cycling trails that crisscross through the reserve, allowing you to immerse yourself in nature. Keep an eye out for kingfishers, herons, and other water-loving bird species as you stroll along the riverbanks. The Nidda Nature Reserve is also home to an array of wildlife, including otters, beavers, and various species of fish.

Frankfurt Zoo

While not a natural reserve, the Frankfurt Zoo provides a unique opportunity to observe and learn about wildlife from around the world. Located in Frankfurt's Ostend district, the zoo is home to over 4,500 animals, representing more than 450 species. From majestic elephants and big cats to playful primates and colorful birds, the Frankfurt Zoo offers a diverse and educational experience for visitors of all ages. The zoo also participates in various breeding and conservation programs, contributing to the preservation of endangered species.

Botanical Gardens

In addition to its wildlife, Frankfurt is also blessed with beautiful botanical gardens that showcase a wide variety of plant species. The Palmengarten, one of the largest botanical gardens in Germany, boasts an impressive collection of exotic plants and stunning themed gardens. Wander through lush tropical greenhouses, explore aromatic herb gardens, or relax in serene Japanese landscapes. The Botanical Garden of Goethe University is another notable green oasis in the city, featuring a range of plant species from different climates and regions.

Environmental Education and Awareness

Frankfurt places a strong emphasis on environmental education and awareness, offering numerous educational programs, workshops, and guided tours focused on nature conservation and wildlife protection. These initiatives aim to foster an understanding of the importance of biodiversity and sustainable practices among residents and visitors alike.

In conclusion, Frankfurt's commitment to preserving its natural heritage is evident through its national parks, nature reserves, and wildlife conservation efforts. Whether you choose to explore the sprawling landscapes of the Odenwald or Taunus Nature Parks, observe rare bird species in the Rhine-Main Biosphere Reserve, or immerse yourself in the diverse plant life of the botanical gardens, Frankfurt offers a range of experiences for nature lovers. So, embark on a journey of discovery and connect with the wild side of Frankfurt as you explore its national parks and wildlife habitats.

Survival Guide

To ensure that your trip is smooth, enjoyable, and stress-free, here's a comprehensive survival guide to help you navigate Frankfurt and make the most of your time there.

Summer

Summer in Frankfurt is a delightful season when the city comes alive with a vibrant atmosphere, outdoor activities, and a multitude of cultural events. From enjoying sunny days in the parks to exploring the city's rich history and indulging in delicious cuisine, there's something for everyone to savor during the summer months.

Outdoor Exploration

With longer days and pleasant weather, summer is the perfect time to explore

Frankfurt's green spaces and outdoor attractions. The Palmengarten, a stunning botanical garden, is in full bloom, offering a feast for the senses with its vibrant flowers, exotic plants, and tranquil pathways. The English Garden, located near the city center, is an idyllic spot for picnics, leisurely walks, or simply basking in the sunshine. You can also venture further afield to the Taunus Mountains or the Odenwald Forest for hiking, biking, or even a refreshing swim in the natural lakes and rivers.

River Cruises

The Main River is an integral part of Frankfurt's charm, and during summer, river cruises are a popular way to experience the city from a different perspective. Hop aboard a leisurely boat tour and sail along the Main, taking in the panoramic views of the city skyline, the historic bridges, and the lush riverbanks. Some cruises even offer dining options, allowing you to enjoy a delicious meal while cruising along the river.

Festivals and Open-Air Events

Summer in Frankfurt is synonymous with a vibrant festival scene. From music festivals to cultural events, there's no shortage of entertainment to enjoy. The Museumsuferfest, held in August, is a highlight of the summer calendar, where the banks of the Main River transform into a lively celebration of music, art, and culinary delights. The Palmengarten Sommerfest offers a unique blend of music, dance, and theater performances in the enchanting setting of the botanical garden. Additionally, open-air cinema screenings, concerts, and street festivals are held throughout the city, adding to the festive atmosphere.

Al Fresco Dining

One of the joys of summer in Frankfurt is dining outdoors and savoring the local cuisine. Many restaurants and cafes set up charming outdoor seating areas where you can enjoy your meal while soaking up the sunshine. From traditional German beer gardens to international eateries with sidewalk terraces, there are endless options to satisfy your taste buds. Indulge in local specialties such as grilled sausages, potato salad, and refreshing apple wine, or explore the diverse culinary scene offering international flavors from around the world.

Cultural Delights

Frankfurt's cultural scene thrives during the summer months, offering a rich array of art exhibitions, performances, and cultural events. Visit the Städel Museum, one of Germany's most renowned art museums, to admire masterpieces from various eras, or explore contemporary art at the Museum of Modern Art (MMK). The Opera House hosts captivating performances, from classic operas to modern ballets, while theaters across the city showcase plays, musicals, and experimental performances. Be sure to check the summer schedules for special outdoor performances, concerts, and theater productions held in parks and squares.

Shopping and Sales

Summer in Frankfurt also means the start of the summer sales season, making it an ideal time for shopping enthusiasts. Take advantage of discounted prices and explore the city's shopping districts, from the bustling Zeil shopping street to luxury boutiques on Goethestraße. Fashion, accessories, home decor, and more can be found in a wide range of stores, including department stores, fashion chains, and local boutiques.

Day Trips

While Frankfurt has plenty to offer, summer provides an excellent opportunity to take day trips and explore the surrounding areas. Just a short distance from the city center, you can visit charming towns such as Wiesbaden, known for its elegant architecture and thermal baths, or Mainz, with its historic Old Town and famous Gutenberg Museum. The picturesque Rhine Valley is also within reach, where you can embark on a scenic river cruise, visit medieval castles, or explore charming wine villages. If you're seeking nature and outdoor adventures, consider a trip to the Rhine-Main Nature Park or the Vogelsberg Mountains, both offering beautiful landscapes and opportunities for hiking, biking, and nature exploration.

Summer Markets

Summer brings an abundance of markets to Frankfurt, offering a vibrant atmosphere and a variety of local products. The weekly farmers' markets showcase fresh produce, regional specialties, artisanal products, and flowers. Visit the Konstablerwache Market, one of the largest in the city, to immerse yourself in the bustling atmosphere and sample delicious local treats. Additionally, summer flea markets and craft markets pop up throughout the city, providing a treasure trove of unique finds, vintage items, and handmade crafts.

Sports and Recreation

Make the most of the summer weather by engaging in outdoor sports and recreational activities. Frankfurt offers numerous opportunities for sports enthusiasts, including jogging or cycling along the scenic riverfront paths, playing beach volleyball in designated areas, or joining outdoor fitness classes in the parks. The city's public swimming pools and lakes are perfect for cooling off and enjoying a refreshing swim. You can also rent paddleboats or kayaks to explore the Main River at your own pace.

Beer Gardens and Wine Bars

Germany is renowned for its beer culture, and Frankfurt has its fair share of traditional beer gardens where you can relax and socialize. Enjoy a cold beer under the shade of chestnut trees while savoring traditional German dishes. If you prefer wine, Frankfurt's proximity to the Rheingau region means you can indulge in local wines at cozy wine bars and taverns. Try the region's famous Riesling wines or explore other varietals produced in the surrounding vineyards.

Music and Concerts

Summer evenings in Frankfurt are often accompanied by live music and open-air concerts. Various parks and squares throughout the city host outdoor performances featuring local bands, jazz ensembles, and classical orchestras. The Opernplatz Festival, held in July, showcases a diverse range of musical genres and is a highlight for music lovers. Additionally, many bars and clubs have outdoor stages or rooftop terraces where you can enjoy live music while taking in the city views.

Escape to Nature

If you're seeking a break from the city's hustle and bustle, Frankfurt's proximity to nature allows for easy escapes into tranquil landscapes. The nearby Taunus Mountains provide ample opportunities for hiking, mountain biking, or simply enjoying a peaceful picnic surrounded by lush forests and picturesque views. Explore nature reserves such as the Schwanheimer Düne, a unique sand dune habitat, or the Frankfurt Green Belt, a stretch of protected nature areas and meadows perfect for leisurely walks and birdwatching.

Remember to stay hydrated and protect yourself from the sun during the summer months. Whether you're exploring the city's cultural delights, enjoying outdoor activities, or simply relaxing in the parks, Frankfurt in the summer offers a vibrant and captivating experience that will leave you with wonderful memories.

Winter

Winter in Frankfurt transforms the city into a charming winter wonderland, offering a unique and magical experience for visitors. Here is a detailed exploration of what you can expect during the winter season in Frankfurt:

Festive Markets

One of the highlights of winter in Frankfurt is the renowned Christmas Market, known as the Frankfurter Weihnachtsmarkt. This traditional market takes place in the heart of the city and attracts millions of visitors each year. Stroll through the festively decorated stalls, admire the sparkling lights, and immerse yourself in the festive atmosphere. Indulge in traditional treats like gingerbread, roasted chestnuts, and mulled wine, and browse the stalls for handmade crafts, ornaments, and unique gifts.

Ice Skating

Embrace the winter spirit by lacing up your skates and gliding across the ice at one of Frankfurt's ice skating rinks. The city offers several outdoor ice rinks, including the Eiserner Steg Ice Rink, located near the city center and offering stunning views of the Main River. Whether you're a beginner or an experienced skater, ice skating is a fun activity for all ages and a great way to enjoy the winter season.

Museum Exploration

Winter provides the perfect opportunity to delve into Frankfurt's rich cultural scene and explore its world-class museums. Seek refuge from the chilly weather and spend your days wandering through the exhibits of the Städel Museum, which houses an impressive collection of European art, or the Museum of Modern Art (MMK), showcasing contemporary works. Immerse yourself in history at the Historical Museum or learn about the city's iconic writer at the Goethe House.

Cozy Cafes and Restaurants

Escape the winter chill and warm up in one of Frankfurt's cozy cafes and restaurants. Take a break from exploring and indulge in a cup of hot chocolate, accompanied by a slice of traditional German cake or pastry. Relax in the inviting atmosphere, enjoy the aroma of freshly brewed coffee, and savor the comfort of delicious local cuisine. Frankfurt's culinary scene offers a variety of options, from traditional German fare to international cuisine, ensuring there's something to satisfy every palate.

Opera and Theater Performances

Winter is the perfect time to immerse yourself in the arts and enjoy a performance at one of Frankfurt's esteemed theaters or opera houses. The Frankfurt Opera offers a diverse program of classical operas, ballets, and concerts, while the Schauspiel Frankfurt presents a range of theatrical productions. Immerse yourself in the world of performing arts and witness captivating performances that will transport you to different eras and realms of imagination.

Winter Walks and Gardens

Despite the cooler temperatures, winter in Frankfurt can be a beautiful time for leisurely walks and exploring the city's parks and gardens. Bundle up and wander through the Palmengarten, a botanical garden that features tropical greenhouses and serene winter landscapes. Enjoy the tranquility of the Nizza Park, where you can stroll along tree-lined paths or find a bench to admire the scenic views. Frankfurt's parks offer a peaceful retreat amidst the winter scenery.

New Year's Eve Celebrations

As the year comes to a close, Frankfurt comes alive with vibrant New Year's Eve celebrations. Join the crowds at the Römerberg, the city's historic square, where fireworks light up the sky at midnight. Enjoy live music, street performances, and festive food stalls as you bid farewell to the old year and welcome in the new. Alternatively, you can choose to celebrate at one of the city's restaurants, bars, or clubs, where special events and parties take place to mark the occasion.

Day Trips to Nearby Destinations

While Frankfurt itself offers a plethora of winter activities, its central location makes it an ideal base for day trips to nearby destinations. Take advantage of the winter season to explore the surrounding areas and discover the winter beauty of the region. Here are a few suggestions for day trips from Frankfurt:

- **Rüdesheim am Rhein:** Embark on a scenic journey along the Rhine River and visit the charming town of Rüdesheim am Rhein. Explore the narrow streets lined with half-timbered houses, visit the famous Drosselgasse with its lively atmosphere, and enjoy panoramic views from the Niederwald Monument. Don't miss the opportunity to sample the region's renowned

Riesling wines and indulge in a cozy meal at a local tavern.

- **b. Heidelberg:** Just a short train ride away from Frankfurt, Heidelberg is a picturesque city known for its romantic charm. Explore the historic Heidelberg Castle, stroll along the Philosopher's Walk for breathtaking views of the city, and wander through the old town's cobblestone streets lined with shops and cafes. The winter ambiance adds a touch of enchantment to Heidelberg's already captivating atmosphere.
- **c. Wiesbaden:** Discover the neighboring city of Wiesbaden, known for its elegant architecture, thermal baths, and vibrant cultural scene. Take a leisurely walk through the city center, admire the grand buildings of the Kurhaus and the State Theatre, and relax in one of the luxurious thermal spas. Enjoy a shopping spree along the bustling Wilhelmstrasse, known for its designer boutiques and upscale shops.

- **d. Taunus Mountains:** Embrace the winter scenery by venturing into the Taunus Mountains, located just outside of Frankfurt. Enjoy outdoor activities such as hiking or cross-country skiing in the pristine forests, take in panoramic views from the Feldberg summit, or visit the charming villages nestled in the mountains. The tranquil beauty of the Taunus Mountains offers a peaceful escape from the city.
- **e. Mainz:** Explore the historic city of Mainz, situated on the banks of the Rhine River. Visit the Mainz Cathedral, known for its stunning Romanesque architecture, and explore the Gutenberg Museum to learn about the city's connection to Johannes Gutenberg and the printing press. Stroll along the colorful lanes of the old town, browse through antique shops, and indulge in

local delicacies at traditional wine taverns.

Remember to check the schedules and availability of transportation options for your chosen day trips, as some attractions may have adjusted opening hours during the winter season. Dress warmly, wear comfortable shoes, and be prepared for changing weather conditions during your excursions.

Winter in Frankfurt offers a delightful blend of festive traditions, cultural experiences, and picturesque landscapes. Whether you choose to explore the city's vibrant events, savor cozy moments in cafes, or venture into the surrounding areas, you're sure to create lasting memories in this enchanting winter destination.

Spring

As winter fades away, Frankfurt, the dynamic metropolis in the heart of Germany, welcomes the arrival of spring with open arms. This enchanting season brings a burst of life and color to the city, offering residents and visitors a multitude of delightful experiences. From blooming gardens and outdoor activities to cultural events and festivals, Frankfurt during springtime is a true celebration of nature, art, and community.

Blooming Gardens and Parks

One of the most captivating aspects of spring in Frankfurt is the transformation of its gardens and parks into veritable havens of beauty. The city boasts several stunning green spaces where locals and tourists alike can immerse themselves in the wonders of nature. The Palmengarten, a botanical garden spanning 22 hectares, dazzles visitors with its vibrant array of flowers, trees, and exotic plants. Strolling through its themed gardens, such as the Mediterranean terraces or the rose garden, is a sensory delight.

Another beloved destination is the Gruneburgpark, located near the Goethe University. This picturesque park features lush green lawns, meandering paths, and enchanting cherry blossom trees. As spring takes hold, the cherry blossoms burst into bloom, creating a breathtaking spectacle of delicate pink petals that attract countless admirers. It's a perfect spot for picnics, leisurely walks, or simply finding a peaceful retreat amidst the city's hustle and bustle.

Outdoor Activities

With the arrival of milder temperatures and longer daylight hours, Frankfurt becomes an ideal playground for outdoor enthusiasts. The city offers an abundance of opportunities to engage in recreational activities and enjoy the rejuvenating spirit of spring. The Main River, which flows through the heart of Frankfurt, provides a picturesque backdrop for activities such as boat tours, kayaking, or simply strolling along the riverbank. Renting a bike and exploring the city's extensive network of cycling paths is another popular choice for locals and tourists alike.

For those seeking a tranquil escape, the nearby Taunus Mountains offer breathtaking natural landscapes just a short distance from the city. Hiking trails wind through lush forests, leading to panoramic viewpoints that offer stunning vistas of the surrounding countryside. Springtime in the Taunus Mountains is particularly magical, as wildflowers carpet the meadows, and the air is filled with the sweet scent of blossoming trees.

Cultural Events and Festivals

Frankfurt's vibrant cultural scene comes alive during the spring months, with an array of events and festivals that showcase the city's rich heritage and artistic flair. The Museum

Embankment Festival, held in August, is a highlight of Frankfurt's cultural calendar. This open-air festival takes place along the banks of the Main River, attracting visitors from far and wide. Museums, galleries, and cultural institutions participate in the festival, offering special exhibitions, performances, and concerts.

In addition to the Museum Embankment Festival, spring in Frankfurt hosts a variety of other cultural events. The Dippemess, a traditional fair with roots dating back to the 14th century, offers a lively atmosphere with amusement rides, games, and delicious street food. The Frankfurt Book Fair, held in October, is one of the world's largest book fairs and attracts publishers, authors, and literary enthusiasts from across the globe.

Spring in Frankfurt is a time of transformation, when the city emerges from the grasp of winter and bursts into life. The blooming gardens, vibrant parks, and abundance of outdoor activities create an inviting atmosphere that entices both residents and visitors. Coupled with the city's rich cultural offerings and exciting festivals, Frankfurt in spring is a truly enchanting destination.

Accommodation

Frankfurt, as a bustling international hub and financial center, offers a diverse range of accommodation options to suit the needs and preferences of every traveler. Whether you're seeking luxury, comfort, convenience, or budget-friendly choices, Frankfurt has something to offer. From world-class hotels to charming boutique accommodations and affordable guesthouses, here's a detailed overview of the different types of lodging available in the city.

Luxury Hotels

For those seeking the epitome of comfort and luxury, Frankfurt boasts a selection of renowned five-star hotels. These establishments offer impeccable service, elegant interiors, and a host of amenities to ensure a truly memorable stay. Many luxury hotels in Frankfurt are located in the city center, close to major attractions, shopping districts, and business centers. These hotels often feature exquisite restaurants, wellness facilities, spas, and panoramic views of the city skyline. Some of the prominent luxury hotels in Frankfurt include the Jumeirah Frankfurt, Steigenberger Frankfurter Hof, and The Westin Grand Frankfurt.

Business Hotels

Given Frankfurt's status as a major financial and business hub, it's no surprise that the city offers a wide range of business-oriented hotels. These accommodations are designed to cater to the needs of business travelers, providing amenities such as conference facilities, executive lounges, high-speed internet access, and convenient locations near business districts. Many business hotels in Frankfurt also offer additional services such as business centers, meeting rooms, and dedicated concierge services. Some notable options in this category include the Hilton Frankfurt City Centre, NH Collection Frankfurt City, and InterContinental Frankfurt.

Boutique Hotels

If you're looking for a unique and intimate experience, Frankfurt's boutique hotels offer a charming alternative to larger chain establishments. These smaller, independently-owned hotels often feature stylish and individually decorated rooms, creating a distinctive ambiance that reflects the character of the city. Boutique hotels in Frankfurt can be found in various neighborhoods, from the city center to more residential areas, providing a more personalized and authentic stay. Some noteworthy boutique hotels include Hotel

Cult Frankfurt City, Villa Kennedy - a Rocco Forte Hotel, and 25hours Hotel the Goldman.

Budget-Friendly Options

Travelers on a budget need not worry, as Frankfurt also offers a range of affordable accommodation options without compromising on quality and comfort. Budget-friendly hotels, guesthouses, and hostels can be found throughout the city, catering to backpackers, solo travelers, and families seeking affordable stays. These accommodations typically offer clean and comfortable rooms, communal areas, and basic amenities at wallet-friendly prices. Hostels such as Five Elements Hostel, United Hostel Frankfurt City Center, and A&O Frankfurt Galluswarte provide a sociable atmosphere and are popular choices among budget-conscious travelers.

Alternative Accommodations:

In recent years, alternative accommodation options have gained popularity in Frankfurt, providing unique and often more affordable choices. Vacation rentals, serviced apartments, and homestays can be booked through various online platforms, offering a home-away-from-home experience. These options are particularly suitable for families or longer stays, as they provide additional space, kitchen facilities, and the opportunity to immerse you in the local neighborhood. Platforms like Airbnb, Booking.com, and HomeAway offer a wide range of alternative accommodations in Frankfurt.

Frankfurt's accommodation options cater to a diverse range of travelers, offering luxury, comfort, convenience, and affordability. Whether you're seeking a lavish hotel experience, a charming boutique stay, a budget-friendly option, or the comforts of a home-like environment, Frankfurt has a wealth of choices to suit your preferences and budget. With its world-class hospitality and a wide variety of accommodations, Frankfurt ensures that every visitor can find a place to stay that meets their needs while enjoying the city's vibrant atmosphere and rich

Electricity

When visiting Frankfurt, it's essential to understand the electricity system to ensure a seamless experience with your electronic devices. Here's some detailed information about the voltage, plugs, and power standards in Frankfurt:

Voltage

In Frankfurt, the standard voltage is 230 volts, and the frequency is 50 hertz. This voltage level is common throughout Europe, so if your devices are compatible with this range, you won't require a voltage converter. However, if your electrical devices are designed for a different voltage (e.g., 110-120V in North America), you will need a voltage converter to prevent damage to your devices.

Plugs and Sockets

The plug type used in Frankfurt and Germany, in general, is the Europlug (Type C) and the Schuko plug (Type F). These plugs have two or three round pins and are compatible with most European countries. The Europlug has two pins, while the Schuko plug has two pins with an additional grounding pin. It's advisable to carry a universal travel adapter or an adapter specifically designed for Europe to ensure compatibility with the local outlets.

Power Standards

Frankfurt operates on the European standard for power outlets, which provides alternating current (AC). The standard power supply is 50 hertz. Most electronic devices, including laptops, smartphones, and camera chargers, can handle this frequency without any issues. However, it's always a good idea to check the power requirements of your specific devices before plugging them in.

Power Interruptions:

Electricity supply in Frankfurt is generally reliable and stable. Power outages are infrequent, but they can occur due to maintenance work or unforeseen circumstances. In the rare event of a power interruption, it's advisable to have backup power solutions, such as portable power banks for your electronic devices or battery-powered lights.

Adapters and Converters

To ensure your electronic devices can be plugged into Frankfurt's power outlets, it's recommended to carry a suitable travel adapter. A travel adapter allows you to physically connect your device's plug to the local outlet configuration. However, keep in mind that a travel adapter only adjusts the physical connection and does not convert voltage. If your devices require a different voltage than what is provided in Frankfurt, you will also need a voltage converter to avoid damage.

Purchasing Electronics and Chargers

If you need to purchase electronics or chargers while in Frankfurt, you'll find a wide selection available at electronics stores, department stores, and specialized retailers. The city offers a variety of options to cater to different budgets and requirements. It's advisable to check the voltage specifications of the devices you plan to purchase, ensuring they are compatible with your home country's electrical system.

Understanding the electricity standards in Frankfurt is crucial to ensure a smooth and hassle-free experience with your electronic devices. Remember that the voltage in Frankfurt is 230 volts, the plug types are Europlug (Type C) and Schuko plug (Type F), and the power supply is AC with a frequency of 50 hertz. Carrying a suitable travel adapter and, if necessary, a voltage converter will allow you to safely use your devices and enjoy your time in Frankfurt without any electrical complications.

Health

Frankfurt, as a major city in Germany, offers a comprehensive range of healthcare services and wellness facilities to ensure the well-being of both residents and visitors. Here's detailed information about medical services, pharmacies, emergency care, and wellness options in Frankfurt:

Medical Services

Frankfurt is home to numerous hospitals, clinics, and medical centers that provide a wide array of healthcare services. These establishments offer state-of-the-art facilities, advanced medical technology, and highly skilled healthcare professionals. The medical services available in Frankfurt encompass various specialties, including general medicine, specialized surgery, pediatrics, gynecology, dermatology, and more. Some prominent hospitals and medical centers in Frankfurt include the University Hospital Frankfurt, Frankfurt Hospital, and St. Catherine Hospital Frankfurt.

Pharmacies

Pharmacies, known as "Apotheke" in German, are readily available throughout Frankfurt. These pharmacies offer prescription medications, over-the-counter drugs, and various health-related products. In Germany, it's common for pharmacies to operate during regular business hours, with some having extended hours or 24-hour service on a rotating basis. In case of emergencies or after-hours needs, there is usually one or more pharmacies designated as "Notdienst" that provide service outside regular hours. These designated pharmacies can be found on a sign displayed at every pharmacy or by checking the local listings.

Emergency Care

In case of a medical emergency, Frankfurt has a well-developed emergency care system. The emergency telephone number in Germany, including Frankfurt, is 112, which connects you to the emergency services (ambulance, fire department, and police). The emergency medical services in Frankfurt are highly efficient and can provide immediate medical assistance in urgent situations. It's important to note that emergency medical services are generally free of charge, regardless of insurance status, ensuring that anyone in need can access immediate medical attention.

Wellness Facilities

Frankfurt offers a variety of wellness facilities to promote overall well-being and relaxation. These facilities range from luxurious spas and wellness centers to fitness clubs and yoga studios. Spa and wellness centers provide a range of services, including massages, facials, body treatments, saunas, and steam baths, allowing visitors to unwind and rejuvenate. Fitness clubs and yoga studios offer a diverse selection of exercise classes, gym equipment, and personal training options to cater to different fitness preferences.

Health Insurance

If you are a visitor to Frankfurt or Germany, it's important to have appropriate health insurance coverage. The European Health Insurance Card (EHIC) allows citizens of the European Union (EU) to receive necessary medical treatment in Germany. Non-EU citizens are advised to obtain travel health insurance that covers medical expenses during their stay in Frankfurt. It's recommended to check the terms and conditions of your insurance policy to ensure it provides adequate coverage for medical emergencies and treatment in Frankfurt.

Frankfurt offers a comprehensive healthcare infrastructure, including hospitals, clinics, pharmacies, emergency care services, and wellness facilities. Visitors can rely on the availability of medical services, whether for routine check-ups, specialized treatments, or emergencies. Pharmacies are conveniently located, and emergency care can be accessed by dialing 112. Additionally, wellness facilities provide opportunities for relaxation and promoting overall well-being. It's important to have appropriate health insurance coverage to ensure peace of mind during your stay in Frankfurt.

Internet Activities

Frankfurt, as a modern and technologically advanced city, provides a wide range of internet activities and services to keep residents and visitors connected. Whether you need internet access for work, leisure, or staying connected with friends and family, here's a detailed overview of internet options and activities in Frankfurt:

Internet Access

Internet access in Frankfurt is widely available, with various options to suit different needs. Most hotels, cafes, and restaurants in the city provide free Wi-Fi for customers, allowing you to stay connected while enjoying a meal or a cup of coffee. Additionally, many public spaces, such as parks, libraries, and transportation hubs, offer free Wi-Fi hotspots for the convenience of the public. It's advisable to check with your accommodation or the venue you plan to visit for information on their Wi-Fi availability and access procedures.

Mobile Data

If you prefer to have internet access on the go, Frankfurt has excellent mobile network coverage. You can choose from several mobile network providers that offer prepaid SIM cards or mobile data plans. These providers include Deutsche Telekom, Vodafone, and O2. Prepaid SIM cards can be purchased at various outlets, including convenience stores, electronics stores, and mobile network provider shops. Make sure your mobile device is unlocked and compatible with the GSM network used in Germany (usually 900/1800 MHz) to use a local SIM card.

Co-Working Spaces

For digital nomads, freelancers, or those who need a productive workspace, Frankfurt offers a variety of co-working spaces. These spaces provide fully equipped workstations, meeting rooms, and high-speed internet access. Some popular co-working spaces in Frankfurt include TechQuartier, CoWorkPlay, and Mind space Frankfurt. These spaces often foster a vibrant community of professionals, offering networking opportunities and events to connect with like-minded individuals.

Online Entertainment

Frankfurt residents and visitors can indulge in various online entertainment activities. Streaming platforms such as Netflix, Amazon Prime Video, and Disney+ are popular choices for enjoying movies, TV shows, and documentaries. Online gaming enthusiasts can join multiplayer games or participate in e-sports events using their gaming consoles, computers, or mobile devices. Frankfurt's internet infrastructure ensures a reliable and fast connection for a seamless online entertainment experience.

Online Booking and Information

When exploring Frankfurt's attractions, it's convenient to use online booking platforms and information resources. Websites and mobile apps such as TripAdvisor, Booking.com, and Visit Frankfurt allow you to book accommodations, attractions, and tours in advance. You can also access valuable information about city maps, transportation schedules, and local recommendations to enhance your Frankfurt experience.

Virtual Meetings and Conferencing

In an increasingly digital world, virtual meetings and conferencing have become commonplace. Frankfurt offers a robust internet infrastructure that supports video conferencing platforms like Zoom, Microsoft Teams, and Google Meet. Business travelers or remote workers can connect with colleagues, clients, or attend virtual conferences seamlessly, ensuring efficient communication and collaboration from anywhere in the city.

Frankfurt provides a wide range of internet activities and services to keep residents and visitors connected in the digital age. With abundant Wi-Fi hotspots, mobile data options, co-working spaces, online entertainment platforms, and resources for online booking and information, staying connected and accessing the internet is easy and convenient in Frankfurt. Whether you need internet access for work, leisure, or staying connected with loved ones, Frankfurt's digital infrastructure ensures a seamless and enjoyable online experience.

Internet café

Internet cafes provide a convenient and accessible option for individuals who require internet access while traveling or do not have a reliable internet connection at their accommodation. In Frankfurt, you can find a variety of internet cafes that offer computer stations, high-speed internet, and additional services. Here's a detailed overview of internet cafes in Frankfurt:

Location and Accessibility

Internet cafes are scattered throughout Frankfurt, with many of them located near popular tourist areas, business districts, and university campuses. You can easily find them in the city center, near train stations, or in busy commercial areas. The central location of these cafes ensures easy accessibility and convenience for both residents and visitors.

Services and Facilities

Internet cafes in Frankfurt provide computer stations equipped with the necessary software and high-speed internet connections. These stations are available for rent on an hourly basis or in prepaid packages. Some cafes offer additional services such as printing, scanning, and photocopying facilities, allowing you to handle your business or personal needs efficiently. Some internet cafes also provide basic office amenities like desks, chairs, and private cubicles for those requiring a quiet workspace.

Wi-Fi and Personal Devices

In addition to computer stations, many internet cafes in Frankfurt offer Wi-Fi access, allowing customers to connect their personal devices such as laptops, tablets, or smartphones. This flexibility enables individuals to work, browse the web, or communicate online using their own devices while enjoying the cafe's atmosphere and services.

Pricing and Packages

Internet cafes in Frankfurt typically charge an hourly rate or offer prepaid packages with discounted rates for longer usage. Prices may vary depending on the location, services provided, and the duration of usage. It's advisable to check the pricing structure of the specific cafe you choose to ensure it aligns with your needs and budget.

Additional Amenities

Some internet cafes in Frankfurt go beyond providing basic internet access. They may offer amenities such as comfortable seating, a variety of beverages and snacks, and a relaxed atmosphere conducive to work or leisure.

These amenities create a pleasant environment for customers, making the cafe not just a place to surf the web but also a space to socialize, relax, or catch up with friends.

Community and Events

Internet cafes can also serve as community spaces, organizing events or workshops related to technology, gaming, or digital media. These events provide opportunities to connect with like-minded individuals, participate in competitions or collaborative projects, and enhance your knowledge in specific areas of interest. Checking the websites or social media pages of internet cafes can provide information about upcoming events and activities.

Safety and Security

When using public computers connecting personal devices to Wi-Fi networks in internet cafes, it's important to prioritize your online safety and security. Ensure you follow best practices such as logging out of your accounts, avoiding entering sensitive information on shared computers, and using secure connections when accessing sensitive websites (look for "https" in the URL). It's also recommended to have updated antivirus software and be cautious when using public Wi-Fi networks.

Conclusion

Internet cafes in Frankfurt provide a convenient option for individuals seeking internet access, computer stations, and additional services. These cafes are located in accessible areas and offer a range of amenities, pricing options, and even community events. Whether you need to catch up on work, browse the web, connect with friends and family, or simply enjoy a comfortable environment while using the internet, Frankfurt's internet cafes are equipped to meet your needs and provide a reliable connection.

Money and Currency Exchange

When traveling to Frankfurt, it's important to have a good understanding of the local currency, banking facilities, and currency exchange options. Here's a detailed overview of money and currency exchange in Frankfurt:

Currency

The official currency of Germany is the Euro (€). Frankfurt, being a major financial hub, widely accepts Euros for all transactions. The Euro is subdivided into cents, with coins available in denominations of 1, 2, 5, 10, 20, and 50 cents, and banknotes in denominations of €5, €10, €20, €50, €100, €200, and €500. It's advisable to carry a mix of smaller denomination notes and coins for convenience, as some smaller establishments may prefer cash for smaller purchases.

Currency Exchange

Currency exchange services are readily available in Frankfurt. You can exchange foreign currency to Euros at various locations, including banks, currency exchange offices, and some hotels. The exchange rates offered may vary between providers, so it's recommended to compare rates and fees before conducting any currency exchange. It's advisable to exchange currency at reputable establishments to ensure fair rates and avoid scams.

Banks and ATMs

Frankfurt has a well-developed banking system, and you'll find numerous banks and ATMs (Automated Teller Machines) throughout the city. ATMs are widely available and accept most international bank cards, including major credit cards and debit cards linked to the Visa, Mastercard, Maestro, and Cirrus networks. ATMs provide a convenient way to withdraw Euros directly from your account, often offering competitive exchange rates. It's advisable to check with your bank regarding any foreign transaction fees or withdrawal limits that may apply.

Credit Cards

Credit cards are widely accepted in Frankfurt, particularly in hotels, restaurants, and larger retail establishments. Visa and Mastercard are commonly accepted, while American Express and Diners Club may have more limited acceptance. It's always a good idea to carry some cash for smaller establishments or places that may not accept cards. When using your credit card, be cautious of potential card skimming or fraudulent activities and keep an eye on your card during transactions.

Traveler's Checks

While traveler's checks were once a popular form of payment for travelers, they have become less commonly used in recent years. Many establishments, including banks, no longer accept traveler's checks, and it may be challenging to find places to cash them. It's advisable to consider alternative payment methods, such as credit cards or cash, when visiting Frankfurt.

Additional Tips:

Inform your bank or credit card provider about your travel plans to ensure your cards are not blocked for suspicious activity while you are in Frankfurt.

Keep a record of important phone numbers, including your bank's customer service number and the number to report lost or stolen cards, in case of emergencies.

Be cautious when using ATMs in public spaces, and shield your PIN while entering it to protect against potential theft or fraud.

Conclusion

Frankfurt offers a robust banking system and a variety of options for currency exchange and accessing money. The Euro is the official currency, and it's widely accepted throughout the city. Banks, ATMs, and currency exchange offices are easily accessible, providing convenience for visitors to exchange currency or withdraw cash. Credit cards are widely accepted, but it's advisable to carry some cash for smaller establishments or situations where cards may not be accepted. By familiarizing yourself with these currency-related aspects, you can confidently manage your finances during your time in Frankfurt.

Public Holiday

Frankfurt, as a vibrant city in Germany, observes various public holidays throughout the year. These holidays hold cultural, historical, or religious significance and often bring a festive atmosphere to the city. Here's a detailed overview of the public holidays celebrated in Frankfurt:

New Year's Day (Neujahrstag) - January 1st

New Year's Day marks the beginning of the Gregorian calendar year. It is a public holiday in Frankfurt, and many businesses, shops, and government offices remain closed. The holiday is often celebrated with fireworks, gatherings, and various cultural events.

Good Friday (Karfreitag) - The Friday before Easter Sunday

Good Friday commemorates the crucifixion of Jesus Christ. It is a religious holiday and a day of reflection and solemnity for Christians. Many businesses and shops in Frankfurt are closed on Good Friday, although some tourist attractions may remain open.

Easter Monday (Ostermontag) - The day after Easter Sunday

Easter Monday is observed as a public holiday in Frankfurt. It is a time for relaxation and family gatherings. Many people take the opportunity to enjoy outdoor activities, visit parks, or organize Easter egg hunts.

Labor Day (Tag der Arbeit) - May 1st

Labor Day is a public holiday that celebrates the achievements of workers and the labor movement. In Frankfurt, various events, rallies, and demonstrations may take place to highlight workers' rights and social issues. Many businesses and shops are closed on this day.

Ascension Day (Christi Himmelfahrt) - 40 days after Easter

Ascension Day commemorates Jesus Christ's ascension into heaven. It is a religious holiday and a time for Christians to attend church services and spend time with family and friends. Many people in Frankfurt take advantage of the long weekend to travel or engage in outdoor activities.

Whit Monday (Pfingstmontag) - The day after Pentecost Sunday

Whit Monday is a Christian holiday that falls 50 days after Easter Sunday. It is a public holiday in Frankfurt, and many people enjoy a day off from work or school. Families often gather for meals or outdoor activities, and some cultural events may take place in the city.

German Unity Day (Tag der Deutschen Einheit) - October 3rd

German Unity Day celebrates the reunification of East and West Germany in 1990. It is a national holiday and a time to reflect on the country's history and the progress made since reunification. Many events, concerts, and fireworks displays are organized throughout Frankfurt to celebrate this important day.

Christmas Day (Erster Weihnachtstag) - December 25th

Christmas Day is a Christian holiday that commemorates the birth of Jesus Christ. It is a public holiday in Frankfurt, and most businesses, shops, and offices remain closed. Families gather to celebrate with festive meals, exchange gifts, and attend church services.

Boxing Day (Zweiter Weihnachtstag) - December 26th

Boxing Day, also known as St. Stephen's Day, is observed on the day after Christmas Day. It is a public holiday in Frankfurt, and many people use this day for relaxation, visiting friends or family, or participating in outdoor activities.

It's important to note that on public holidays, public transportation schedules may operate on a reduced frequency, and some tourist attractions or shops may have modified opening hours. It's advisable to plan accordingly and check specific schedules and closures in advance.

Conclusion

Frankfurt celebrates a range of public holidays that hold cultural, historical, or religious significance. These holidays offer opportunities for relaxation, reflection, family gatherings, and cultural celebrations. Understanding the public holiday schedule in Frankfurt is important for both residents and visitors to plan their activities and make the most of their time in the city. Whether you choose to participate in cultural events, explore the city's attractions, or simply enjoy some downtime, Frankfurt's public holidays provide a unique flavor to the city's vibrant atmosphere. Make sure to check the specific dates and activities associated with each public holiday when planning your visit to Frankfurt.

Work and Minimum Wage

Frankfurt, as a major economic and financial center, offers a wide range of employment opportunities. Whether you are considering working in the city or simply want to understand the local labor market, here's a detailed overview of work and minimum wage regulations in Frankfurt:

Employment Laws and Regulations

Frankfurt operates within the framework of German labor laws, which provide comprehensive protection for workers. These laws cover various aspects of employment, including working hours, vacation entitlements, termination procedures, and social security contributions. Key legislation includes the Federal Employment Protection Act (Kündigungsschutzgesetz), which safeguards employees against unjustified termination, and the Minimum Wage Act (Mindestlohngesetz), which sets a minimum wage for workers.

Minimum Wage

Germany has a statutory minimum wage, which applies to all employees, including those working in Frankfurt. As of my knowledge cutoff in September 2021, the minimum wage in Germany is €9.60 per hour. However, please note that minimum wage rates can be subject to change, so it's essential to verify the current rate with reliable sources or government websites.

Collective Bargaining Agreements

In Frankfurt, many industries and sectors have collective bargaining agreements (Tarifvertrag) in place. These agreements are negotiated between employers' associations and trade unions, outlining specific terms and conditions of employment, including wages, working hours, and benefits. The terms of these agreements can vary depending on the industry or occupation. It's worth noting that collective bargaining agreements often provide more favorable conditions than the statutory minimums.

Working Hours

Under German law, the standard working week is 40 hours, although many employers offer shorter working hours or flexible work arrangements. Overtime work is generally regulated and subject to additional compensation or time-off. It's important to note that certain industries or occupations may have specific rules regarding working hours, such as shift work or night work.

Employment Contracts and Benefits

Employment contracts in Frankfurt, as in the rest of Germany, are typically in writing and include essential details such as job responsibilities, working hours, compensation, and termination conditions. German labor laws also guarantee various benefits to employees, including paid vacation, sick leave, parental leave, and contributions to social security and healthcare.

Work-Life Balance

Germany, including Frankfurt, places a strong emphasis on work-life balance. The legal framework supports employees' rights to leisure time and family commitments. Flexible work arrangements, such as part-time work or telecommuting, are becoming more common, allowing individuals to better balance their professional and personal lives.

Employment Opportunities

Frankfurt's diverse economy offers employment opportunities across various sectors. The city is particularly known for its financial services industry, with numerous banks, insurance companies, and investment firms headquartered in the city. Additionally, Frankfurt has a strong presence in sectors such as information technology, pharmaceuticals, automotive, logistics, and creative industries. Job seekers can explore job portals, recruitment agencies, and company websites to find employment opportunities in Frankfurt.

Work Permits and Visa Requirements

For individuals planning to work in Frankfurt who are not citizens of the European Union (EU) or the European Economic Area (EEA), it's important to understand the visa and work permit requirements. Non-EU/EEA nationals typically require a work visa or residence permit to work legally in Germany. It is advisable to consult the German embassy or consulate in your home country or the relevant immigration authorities for up-to-date information and guidance.

It's important for job seekers to familiarize themselves with the specific requirements and qualifications needed for their desired positions. Researching and networking within their chosen industries can help individuals gain insights into available job opportunities and enhance their chances of securing employment in Frankfurt.

Additionally, Frankfurt's work culture emphasizes a healthy work-life balance, providing employees with ample leisure time and opportunities for personal development. The city's proximity to natural landscapes, parks, and recreational areas allows residents to engage in outdoor activities and pursue hobbies outside of work.

For individuals seeking work in Frankfurt from outside the EU/EEA, understanding the visa and work permit requirements is crucial. The German authorities provide specific guidelines and regulations for non-EU/EEA nationals, and it is essential to comply with the necessary documentation and procedures to work legally in the city.

Moreover, Frankfurt boasts a strong network of job placement agencies, recruitment services, and online job portals that can assist individuals in finding suitable employment opportunities. It is advisable to utilize these resources, along with professional networks and industry-specific events, to connect with potential employers and expand career prospects.

As the economic landscape evolves, it is essential for job seekers in Frankfurt to stay updated on industry trends, technological advancements, and skill requirements. Acquiring additional qualifications, participating in professional development programs, and maintaining a proactive approach to learning can help individuals stay competitive in the job market and enhance their career progression.

In conclusion, Frankfurt provides a dynamic employment environment with diverse opportunities across multiple sectors. By familiarizing themselves with the labor laws, minimum wage regulations, and employment standards, job seekers can navigate the job market with confidence and make informed decisions about their career paths in the city.

Customs and Regulations

When traveling to Frankfurt, it's important to understand the customs and regulations in place to ensure a smooth and hassle-free experience. Here's a detailed overview of the customs and regulations you should be aware of when visiting Frankfurt:

Entry Requirements

Before traveling to Frankfurt, ensure that you have the necessary travel documents. If you are a citizen of a European Union (EU) or European Economic Area (EEA) country, you only need a valid passport or national identity card for entry. However, if you are a non-EU/EEA citizen, you may require a visa to enter Germany. It's advisable to check the visa requirements and apply well in advance of your trip.

Customs Allowances

When entering Frankfurt from a non-EU country, you are subject to customs regulations regarding duty-free allowances. These allowances specify the maximum quantity of goods, including alcohol, tobacco, and other items, that you can bring into the country without paying customs duties. It's important to familiarize yourself with the specific allowances to avoid any customs-related issues.

Prohibited and Restricted Items

Certain items are prohibited or restricted from being brought into Frankfurt or Germany. These include illegal drugs, weapons, counterfeit goods, and endangered species products. It's crucial to review the list of prohibited and restricted items to avoid any legal repercussions or confiscations at customs.

Currency Regulations

When entering or leaving Frankfurt, there are regulations regarding the amount of currency you can carry. If you are traveling within the European Union, there are generally no restrictions on the amount of currency you can bring. However, if you are traveling from or to a non-EU country, you must declare any amount exceeding €10,000 or its equivalent in another currency.

Transportation of Pets

If you are traveling with pets to Frankfurt, there are specific regulations you must comply with. Pets, such as dogs and cats, need to have a microchip for identification, a valid rabies vaccination certificate, and, in some cases, a pet passport. It's recommended to check the specific requirements for transporting pets to Frankfurt and ensure compliance with the regulations.

Health and Safety Regulations

Frankfurt follows health and safety regulations to ensure the well-being of residents and visitors. It's important to adhere to regulations related to public health, including hygiene standards and food safety. Additionally, it's advisable to have travel insurance to cover any medical emergencies that may arise during your stay.

Smoking Regulations

Germany has smoking regulations in place, and Frankfurt adheres to these laws. Smoking is prohibited in most public buildings, including airports, train stations, restaurants, bars, and shopping centers. Designated smoking areas may be available, but it's important to respect the regulations and be mindful of others.

Data Protection and Privacy

Germany has strict data protection and privacy laws. When using public Wi-Fi or providing personal information, ensure that you are using secure networks and websites. It's important to be cautious and protect your personal data to avoid any privacy breaches.

Environmental Regulations

Frankfurt, like the rest of Germany, places great importance on environmental conservation. Recycling is highly encouraged, and there are separate bins for different types of waste, such as paper, plastic, glass, and organic waste. It's advisable to familiarize yourself with the local recycling guidelines and adhere to them during your stay.

Conclusion

Understanding the customs and regulations in Frankfurt is essential for a smooth and enjoyable visit. By familiarizing yourself with entry requirements, customs allowances, prohibited items, and other regulations, you can ensure compliance and avoid any potential issues. Respecting health and safety regulations, data protection laws, and environmental guidelines will contribute to a positive experience while visiting Frankfurt.

Adventures and outdoors activities

While Frankfurt is known for its bustling cityscape and financial prowess, the region surrounding the city offers a variety of outdoor adventures and activities for nature enthusiasts and adventure seekers. Here's a detailed overview of the adventures and outdoor activities you can experience in and around Frankfurt:

Taunus Mountains

The Taunus Mountains, located just outside of Frankfurt, Germany, are a picturesque mountain range that offers a wide range of outdoor activities and stunning natural beauty. Spanning an area of approximately 2,700 square kilometers, the Taunus

Mountains are a popular destination for both locals and tourists alike.

Hiking and walking enthusiasts will find a plethora of well-marked trails that crisscross the Taunus Mountains. The trails cater to all skill levels, from easy leisurely walks to challenging hikes for the more experienced adventurers. As you explore the mountains, you'll be treated to breathtaking views of rolling hills, dense forests, and charming villages nestled amidst the landscape. The fresh air and tranquil surroundings create a perfect setting for relaxation and rejuvenation.

One of the highlights of the Taunus Mountains is the Feldberg, the highest peak in the range. Standing at an elevation of 879 meters (2,884 feet), the Feldberg offers panoramic views of the surrounding countryside. In winter, the Feldberg transforms into a popular winter sports destination, attracting skiers, snowboarders, and tobogganers. The mountain boasts several ski slopes, cross-country skiing trails, and a snow park for winter sports enthusiasts to enjoy.

The Taunus Mountains are also a paradise for mountain biking enthusiasts. The region offers a network of well-maintained biking trails that wind through the mountains, providing exciting challenges and scenic routes. Whether you're a beginner or an experienced rider, you'll find trails suited to your skill level. As you pedal through the mountains, you'll be rewarded with breathtaking views and the thrill of adventure.

For rock climbing enthusiasts, the Taunus Mountains offer a range of opportunities to test your skills. The rugged cliffs and rock formations provide the perfect backdrop for climbing and bouldering. Whether you're a beginner looking to try out the sport or an experienced climber seeking a challenge, you'll find suitable routes and climbing spots to satisfy your passion for vertical adventures.

Paragliding is another exhilarating activity that you can experience in the Taunus Mountains. Feel the rush of adrenaline as you take to the skies and soar above the mountains, enjoying panoramic views of the breathtaking landscape below. Paragliding schools and experienced instructors are available in the region to ensure a safe and thrilling experience.

In addition to the outdoor activities, the Taunus Mountains are home to charming villages and towns that are worth exploring. These idyllic settlements offer a glimpse into traditional German culture and architecture. You can wander through the streets, visit local shops and cafes, and interact with friendly locals who are proud of their mountainous home.

The Taunus Mountains also boast natural attractions such as beautiful waterfalls, serene lakes, and meandering rivers. These natural wonders provide excellent opportunities for relaxation, photography, and immersing oneself in the tranquil ambiance of the mountains.

Whether you're seeking an adrenaline-pumping adventure or a peaceful retreat in nature, the Taunus Mountains in Frankfurt offer a wealth of opportunities to satisfy your outdoor cravings. With its diverse range of activities, stunning landscapes, and charming villages, the Taunus Mountains are a must-visit destination for nature lovers and adventure seekers alike.

Rhein River

The Rhein River, flowing near Frankfurt, Germany, is one of the most iconic and picturesque waterways in Europe. With its scenic beauty and historical significance, the Rhein River offers a plethora of activities and attractions for locals and visitors alike.

One of the best ways to experience the Rhein River is by embarking on a river cruise. Several companies operate cruises along the river, allowing you to leisurely navigate its waters while taking in the stunning landscapes. From the deck of a cruise ship, you can admire the charming towns, picturesque vineyards, and majestic castles that line the riverbanks. Some cruises also offer informative commentary about the history and culture of the region, providing a deeper understanding of the area's significance.

For a more active experience, kayaking and canoeing on the Rhein River are popular options. Rental services are available, allowing you to explore the river at your own pace and immerse yourself in the tranquility of the water. Paddling along the river offers a unique perspective and allows you to get closer to nature, enjoying the peaceful ambiance and stunning scenery.

The Rhein River is also renowned for its wine production, and a visit to the Rheingau wine region is a must for wine enthusiasts. Located along the banks of the Rhein River, the Rheingau is home to some of Germany's most famous vineyards. You can take guided tours of the vineyards, learn about the winemaking process, and, of course, indulge in wine tastings. The region is particularly known for its Riesling wines, which are highly regarded for their quality and unique flavor profiles.

Additionally, the Rhein River offers opportunities for swimming and sunbathing during the summer months. Several designated swimming areas and beaches can be found along the river, providing a refreshing respite from the city's summer heat. These recreational spots are equipped with facilities such as changing rooms, showers, and picnic areas, making them ideal for a day of relaxation and fun with family and friends.

The Rhein River is also a paradise for cycling enthusiasts. The Rhein Radweg, or Rhein River Cycle Route, is a well-developed cycling path that spans several countries and stretches along the riverbanks. In Frankfurt, you can join the cycle route and pedal alongside the river, enjoying the scenic views and passing through charming towns and villages. Whether you're a leisurely cyclist or a more experienced rider, the Rhein River offers a beautiful backdrop for a cycling adventure.

Festivals and events that take place along the Rhein River add to its vibrant atmosphere. From music festivals to cultural celebrations, there's always something happening along the riverbanks. One notable event is the Rhein in Flammen, a spectacular fireworks display that lights up the night sky. This event takes place in various cities along the river and attracts thousands of visitors who gather to witness the stunning pyrotechnic show.

In conclusion, the Rhein River in Frankfurt offers a multitude of experiences for visitors to enjoy. Whether you choose to embark on a scenic river cruise, explore the vineyards of the Rheingau wine region, engage in water activities like kayaking or canoeing, relax on the river's beaches, cycle along the riverbanks, or participate in vibrant festivals and events, the Rhein River promises an unforgettable and enriching experience for all who visit.

Frankfurt Green Belt

The Frankfurt Green Belt is a vast stretch of protected green spaces and nature reserves that spans over 8,000 hectares, making it one of the largest urban green areas in Germany. Located within the city limits of Frankfurt, it serves as a valuable ecological corridor and a haven for both flora and fauna. The Green

Belt provides residents and visitors with opportunities to connect with nature, enjoy recreational activities, and escape the hustle and bustle of the city.

The Green Belt is a paradise for outdoor enthusiasts, offering a network of walking and hiking trails that wind through its diverse landscapes. As you explore the trails, you'll encounter lush forests, meadows, wetlands, and serene lakes, providing a tranquil escape from urban life. The well-maintained paths cater to all fitness levels, from leisurely strolls to more challenging hikes, allowing everyone to appreciate the natural beauty of the area.

Cycling enthusiasts will also find plenty of opportunities to pedal through the Green Belt. The network of cycling paths offers scenic routes that traverse the green spaces, allowing riders to immerse themselves in the serene surroundings. Biking through the Green Belt provides a unique perspective on Frankfurt's natural heritage and offers a healthier and eco-friendly way to explore the area.

Within the Frankfurt Green Belt, there are several nature reserves that are home to a rich variety of plant and animal species. These protected areas provide habitats for rare and endangered species, contributing to the preservation of biodiversity in the region. Nature lovers can join guided nature walks led by knowledgeable experts to learn more about the local flora and fauna and gain a deeper understanding of the ecological importance of the Green Belt.

The Green Belt features numerous lakes and ponds where visitors can engage in various water activities. Fishing enthusiasts can try their luck in designated fishing spots, while canoeing and kayaking enthusiasts can explore the calm waters and admire the natural beauty from a different perspective. Some lakes even have designated swimming areas where visitors can take a refreshing dip during the summer months.

Picnic areas and barbecue spots are scattered throughout the Green Belt, providing perfect settings for a leisurely outdoor meal or a gathering with friends and family. The open green spaces and shaded areas make it an ideal place to relax, unwind, and enjoy a picnic amidst nature. Many of these areas are equipped with tables, benches, and barbecue facilities, making it convenient for visitors to spend quality time outdoors.

For birdwatchers, the Frankfurt Green Belt is a paradise. The diverse habitats within the green spaces attract a wide range of bird species, making it an excellent destination for bird watching. Binoculars in hand, you can spot various bird species, including herons, kingfishers, woodpeckers, and many others. Bird watching hides and observation platforms are available in strategic locations, providing vantage points to observe and appreciate the avian residents of the Green Belt.

The Frankfurt Green Belt also serves as a venue for various outdoor events and cultural activities. Concerts, theater performances, and art exhibitions take place in designated areas within the green spaces, creating a unique fusion of nature and culture. These events allow visitors to immerse themselves in the arts while surrounded by the serene beauty of the Green Belt.

In conclusion, the Frankfurt Green Belt is a remarkable natural asset within the city, offering a diverse range of recreational activities, opportunities to connect with nature, and a sanctuary for wildlife. Whether you're seeking a peaceful walk, a bike ride through scenic landscapes, bird watching, a picnic with loved ones, or an outdoor cultural event, the Green Belt provides a welcome respite from the urban environment, allowing you to recharge and reconnect with the beauty of the natural world

Opel Zoo

Opel Zoo, located in Kronberg, just outside of Frankfurt, is a popular destination for families and animal lovers. Spanning over 27 hectares, the zoo is home to a wide variety of animal species from around the world, providing an educational and entertaining experience for visitors of all ages.

As you explore the Opel Zoo, you'll encounter animals from different continents, including mammals, birds, reptiles, and amphibians. The zoo's diverse collection includes elephants, giraffes, lions, tigers, zebras, penguins, monkeys, and many more. The spacious enclosures and naturalistic habitats prioritize the well-being and comfort of the animals, allowing them to exhibit their natural behaviors.

The zoo offers informative and entertaining shows and presentations, providing visitors with the opportunity to learn more about the animals and their habitats. Watch as the zookeepers feed and interact with the animals, and listen to their fascinating stories and conservation efforts. These shows offer insights into the animals' behavior, diet, and conservation status, raising awareness about the importance of protecting wildlife and their habitats.

Opel Zoo provides unique behind-the-scenes experiences and animal encounters, allowing visitors to get up close and personal with some of the residents. Participate in feeding sessions, where you can help feed certain animals and learn more about their dietary needs. You may even have the chance to touch or interact with some of the animals under the supervision of experienced zoo staff.

The zoo's beautifully landscaped grounds offer a pleasant setting for leisurely strolls and picnics. Well-maintained paths guide you through lush gardens, serene ponds, and scenic landscapes. Enjoy the fresh air, soak in the natural beauty, and find peaceful spots to relax and rejuvenate amidst nature. There are designated picnic areas where you can enjoy a meal or snack while surrounded by the sounds of nature.

Opel Zoo is committed to conservation and education, with a focus on raising awareness about endangered species and promoting their preservation. The zoo participates in breeding programs for endangered animals, contributing to their survival and genetic diversity. Informational displays, signs, and interactive exhibits provide valuable insights into the challenges facing wildlife and the importance of conservation efforts.

The zoo offers various amenities to enhance visitors' experiences. There are several cafes and restaurants on-site where you can grab a bite to eat or enjoy a refreshing beverage. Souvenir shops provide opportunities to purchase animal-themed merchandise and support the zoo's conservation initiatives. Additionally, the zoo organizes special events and activities throughout the year, such as themed days, seasonal celebrations, and educational programs for children.

Opel Zoo is easily accessible from Frankfurt, making it a convenient day trip for families and animal enthusiasts. Whether you're seeking an educational experience, a fun-filled day with the family, or a chance to connect with wildlife, Opel Zoo offers a memorable and enriching visit. It serves as a place of entertainment, learning, and appreciation for the diverse wonders of the animal kingdom, fostering a deeper understanding and respect for the natural world.

Outdoor Sports

Frankfurt offers a wide range of outdoor sports and recreational activities, catering to both sports enthusiasts and those looking to stay active and enjoy the outdoors. With its extensive parklands, rivers, and sports facilities, there are plenty of opportunities to engage in various outdoor sports in the city.

Cycling is a popular outdoor activity in Frankfurt, thanks to its well-developed network of cycling paths and scenic routes. The city boasts over 500 kilometers of dedicated cycling paths that crisscross the urban landscape, making it easy to explore the city and its surroundings on two wheels. Whether you prefer leisurely bike rides along the riverbanks or more challenging routes through the countryside, Frankfurt offers options for cyclists of all skill levels.

Golf enthusiasts will find several golf courses in and around Frankfurt where they can practice their swings. These courses feature well-maintained fairways, challenging holes, and beautiful surroundings. Golf clubs in the area often provide facilities such as driving ranges, practice greens, and golf lessons for players of all levels. Whether you're a beginner or an experienced golfer, you can enjoy a round of golf while taking in the scenic landscapes.

Tennis and squash enthusiasts have access to numerous courts throughout Frankfurt. Whether you prefer a friendly match with friends or more competitive play, you'll find well-maintained courts available for rent in sports clubs, parks, and recreational centers. Many facilities offer equipment rental and even coaching services for those looking to improve their game.

Frankfurt is also an excellent city for water sports. The Main River provides opportunities for activities such as kayaking, canoeing, and paddle boarding. Rental services are available along the riverbanks, allowing you to explore the city's waterways and enjoy a unique perspective of the urban landscape. Water sports enthusiasts can also join clubs and organizations that offer training, group outings, and competitions.

For those who enjoy running or jogging, Frankfurt offers a variety of scenic routes and trails. The city's parks, such as the Nidda Park and the Frankfurt City Forest, provide a peaceful and green setting for outdoor workouts. The Main River promenade is another popular spot for runners, offering a flat and picturesque path along the water. Additionally, Frankfurt hosts several running events and marathons throughout the year, providing opportunities to challenge yourself and participate in the vibrant running community.

Other outdoor sports and activities in Frankfurt include basketball, beach volleyball, and football (soccer). Many parks and sports facilities have designated courts and fields where you can gather with friends or join local leagues for friendly matches or more competitive play. Some parks also have outdoor fitness equipment and exercise stations for those looking to incorporate strength training and calisthenics into their outdoor workouts.

In conclusion, Frankfurt offers a wide range of outdoor sports and recreational activities for residents and visitors. Whether you prefer cycling along scenic paths, teeing off at a golf course, engaging in water sports on the Main River, or enjoying a friendly match of tennis or football, the city provides ample opportunities to stay active and enjoy the outdoors. With its beautiful parks, well-maintained facilities, and a vibrant sports community, Frankfurt is a haven for outdoor sports enthusiasts.

Goethe Forest

Goethe Forest, also known as Grüneburgpark, is a peaceful and picturesque urban park located in the heart of Frankfurt. Named after the renowned German writer

Johann Wolfgang von Goethe, the park spans approximately 29 hectares and provides a serene oasis amidst the bustling city.

As you enter Goethe Forest, you'll be greeted by winding paths that lead you through a tranquil landscape of lush greenery, towering trees, and beautiful gardens. The park's well-maintained trails are perfect for a leisurely stroll, a jog, or a peaceful bike ride. The serene atmosphere and natural surroundings make it an ideal escape from the urban hustle and a place to connect with nature.

One of the park's highlights is the botanical garden, which showcases a wide variety of plants and flowers. Take a leisurely walk through the garden to admire the vibrant colors and fragrances. The botanical garden features different themed sections, such as rose gardens, herb gardens, and ornamental flowerbeds, creating a visual feast for nature lovers.

Goethe Forest is not only a haven for flora but also a sanctuary for wildlife. As you explore the park, keep an eye out for the diverse array of bird species that inhabit the area. Binoculars in hand, you can spot different birds, including woodpeckers, sparrows, and robins, among others. Bird watching enthusiasts will find several designated areas and quiet spots where they can observe and appreciate the feathered residents of the forest.

The park offers various amenities to enhance visitors' experiences. Open spaces with well-manicured lawns provide perfect spots for picnics or relaxation. You can spread out a blanket and enjoy a picnic with family or friends while surrounded by the sounds of nature. The park also has designated barbecue areas, allowing visitors to savor a grilled meal amidst the serene surroundings.

For those seeking activities beyond leisurely walks, Goethe Forest offers sports facilities such as tennis courts and a mini-golf course.

These amenities provide opportunities for friendly matches or competitive games. The park also has playgrounds for children, equipped with swings, slides, and climbing structures, ensuring a fun-filled experience for families.

Throughout the year, Goethe Forest hosts various events and cultural activities. Concerts, art exhibitions, and theater performances take place in designated areas within the park, creating a unique fusion of nature and culture. These events allow visitors to enjoy the arts while surrounded by the park's tranquil beauty.

Goethe Forest's central location makes it easily accessible from different parts of the city. Whether you're a local resident looking for a peaceful retreat or a visitor seeking a moment of tranquility, Goethe Forest offers a serene and picturesque escape. It invites you to unwind, reconnect with nature, and appreciate the beauty of Frankfurt's green spaces.

Outdoor Festivals and Events

Frankfurt is a vibrant city that hosts a variety of outdoor festivals and events throughout the year. These events showcase the city's rich culture, music scene, culinary delights, and provide opportunities for residents and visitors alike to come together and celebrate. Here are some of the notable outdoor festivals and events in Frankfurt:

Museumsuferfest (Museum Embankment Festival): This annual festival takes place along the banks of the Main River and is one of Frankfurt's largest cultural events. It features a diverse program of art, music, dance, theater, and food, with over 20 museums participating. Visitors can enjoy live performances, exhibitions, food stalls, and fireworks, creating a vibrant and festive atmosphere.

Main fest: Held in August, Main fest is a traditional folk festival that celebrates the city's culture and traditions. It features carnival rides, games, live music, and a colorful parade that winds through the streets of Frankfurt. Visitors can indulge in traditional food and drinks, experience fairground attractions, and immerse themselves in the lively atmosphere.

Fressgass' Fest: Taking place in June, Fressgass' Fest is a culinary extravaganza that transforms the famous shopping street, Fressgass, into an open-air gourmet market. Local restaurants and vendors set up food stalls, offering a wide range of culinary delights, from traditional German dishes to international cuisine. Visitors can sample delicious food, enjoy live music, and browse through artisanal products.

Luminale: Every two years, Frankfurt is illuminated during the Luminale festival, which showcases artistic light installations and projections throughout the city.

Buildings, landmarks, and public spaces are transformed into mesmerizing works of art, creating a magical atmosphere. Visitors can explore the illuminated streets, attend light art exhibitions, and experience the city in a whole new light.

Opernplatzfest: Opernplatzfest is a summer festival that takes place in the beautiful Opernplatz square. It features live music performances, cultural events, and culinary delights. Visitors can relax on the square's terraces, enjoy open-air concerts, and indulge in delicious food and drinks from the various stalls. The festival also offers a vibrant atmosphere for socializing and people-watching.

Ironman European Championship: Frankfurt hosts the prestigious Ironman European Championship, attracting professional athletes and sports enthusiasts from around the world. The event includes a 3.8-kilometer swim in the Langener Waldsee, a 180-kilometer bike ride through the scenic surroundings of Frankfurt, and a marathon run along the River Main. Spectators can cheer on the athletes, soak up the energetic atmosphere, and enjoy the thrill of this iconic triathlon event.

Berger Strassenfest: Located in the trendy neighborhood of Berger Strasse, this lively street festival takes place in August. It features live music performances, street food stalls, art exhibitions, and a flea market. Visitors can stroll along the bustling street, discover unique crafts, taste delicious food from around the world, and enjoy the vibrant atmosphere of this popular neighborhood festival.

These are just a few examples of the many outdoor festivals and events that take place in Frankfurt. The city's diverse cultural scene ensures that there is always something happening, providing opportunities to celebrate, enjoy live performances, savor delicious food, and immerse oneself in the lively spirit of Frankfurt.

Hot Air Balloon Rides

Hot air balloon rides offer a unique and exhilarating way to experience the beauty of Frankfurt and its surrounding areas from a breathtaking perspective. Floating high above the city, you'll have a bird's-eye view of the skyline, the winding rivers, and the picturesque countryside. Here is some detailed information about hot air balloon rides in Frankfurt:

Experience the Thrill: Hot air balloon rides provide an unforgettable adventure that combines the excitement of flight with the tranquility of drifting through the air. As you ascend into the sky, you'll feel a sense of wonder and freedom, surrounded by panoramic views of the cityscape and the natural landscapes that unfold below.

Safety First: Safety is a top priority for hot air balloon operators in Frankfurt. Licensed pilots ensure that all safety protocols are followed, including regular maintenance of the balloon equipment, pre-flight safety briefings, and adherence to weather conditions. Before embarking on your journey, you'll receive detailed instructions on safety procedures and what to expect during the flight.

Stunning Scenery: From the vantage point of a hot air balloon, you'll have the opportunity to admire Frankfurt's iconic landmarks, such as the Frankfurt Cathedral, the Main Tower, and the Römerberg. As you drift over the Main River, you'll witness the interplay between urban architecture and the natural beauty of the surrounding countryside. The scenic landscapes include rolling hills, vineyards, forests, and charming villages, creating a captivating visual tapestry.

Peaceful Serenity: Unlike other forms of aerial transportation, hot air balloon rides offer a serene and peaceful experience. The gentle motion of the balloon and the absence of engine noise provide a calm atmosphere, allowing you to fully immerse yourself in the beauty of your surroundings. The peacefulness of the flight creates an ideal setting for romantic moments, special occasions, or simply a tranquil escape from the bustling city.

Ideal Weather Conditions: Hot air balloon rides are weather-dependent, and optimal conditions are necessary to ensure a safe and enjoyable experience. Mornings are typically the best time for balloon flights, as the air is usually calm and stable. Wind speeds, temperature, and visibility are all factors that the pilot considers before launching the balloon. It's recommended to check with the balloon operator in advance to confirm the weather conditions and availability of flights.

Duration and Route: The duration of a hot air balloon ride in Frankfurt can vary, typically ranging from one to two hours. The exact duration depends on factors such as weather conditions, wind speed, and the chosen route. The flight path may be determined by the wind direction and the pilot's expertise, offering a unique and unpredictable journey each time. Throughout the flight, the pilot provides commentary and points out notable landmarks, enhancing your understanding and appreciation of the region.

Post-Flight Celebrations: After the balloon lands, there is usually a traditional post-flight celebration. This includes a Champagne toast to commemorate the successful journey and toasting to the ancient ballooning tradition. It's an opportunity to reflect on the experience, share stories with fellow passengers, and celebrate the adventure.

Hot air balloon rides in Frankfurt offer a memorable and breathtaking experience that allows you to see the city and its surroundings in a whole new way. Whether you're seeking a romantic outing, a special celebration, or simply an unforgettable adventure, floating above the landscapes of Frankfurt in a hot air balloon promises an extraordinary and awe-inspiring journey.

The Finest Restaurants, Clubs, and Nighttime Delights

Frankfurt is a city known for its vibrant nightlife and culinary scene. Whether you're looking for a fine dining experience, a trendy club, or a cozy bar, Frankfurt has a variety of options to satisfy every taste. Here are some of the finest restaurants, clubs, and nighttime delights in Frankfurt:

Finest Restaurants

Villa Rothschild: Located in nearby Königstein, Villa Rothschild offers an exquisite fine dining experience. The restaurant holds a Michelin star and features an elegant setting, attentive service, and a menu that showcases creative and beautifully presented dishes.

Lafleur: Situated in the heart of Frankfurt, Lafleur is a renowned restaurant that combines innovative cuisine with a sophisticated atmosphere. Led by a talented chef, the restaurant offers a menu inspired by French and Mediterranean flavors, using only the finest seasonal ingredients.

Restaurant Francais: Housed in the elegant Steigenberger Frankfurter Hof hotel, Restaurant Francais is a culinary gem. With its elegant decor, attentive service, and a menu that focuses on modern French cuisine, the restaurant offers a dining experience that is both refined and memorable.

Trendy Clubs

Gibson Club: Located in the city center, Gibson Club is one of Frankfurt's hottest nightlife spots. It features a modern interior, state-of-the-art sound system, and a lineup of renowned DJs spinning the latest electronic and house music. The club attracts a trendy and energetic crowd.

King Kamehameha Club: Situated on the banks of the River Main, King Kamehameha Club offers a unique Hawaiian-inspired atmosphere. With its beach club vibes, tropical cocktails, and a mix of house and Latin beats, this club provides a lively and memorable experience.

Velvet Club: Velvet Club is a stylish venue known for its chic decor, vibrant ambiance, and a mix of hip-hop, R&B, and dance music. It attracts a diverse crowd and hosts regular themed parties and special events.

Nighttime Delights

Long Island Summer Lounge: Overlooking the Main River, Long Island Summer Lounge is a popular spot for relaxed evenings. It offers comfortable lounging areas, refreshing cocktails, and stunning sunset views. This outdoor venue is the perfect place to unwind and enjoy the company of friends or a romantic evening.

Bockenheimer Weinkontor: Located in the trendy Bockenheim district, Bockenheimer Weinkontor is a cozy wine bar with a wide selection of regional and international wines. It offers a relaxed atmosphere, knowledgeable staff, and occasional live music, making it an ideal spot for wine enthusiasts and those looking for a laid-back evening.

The Parlour: Situated in the Alt-Sachsenhausen district, The Parlour is a hidden gem known for its craft cocktails and vintage-inspired decor. The bar offers a speakeasy-style atmosphere, with dim lighting and comfortable seating. It's a perfect place for those seeking a sophisticated and intimate setting.

These are just a few examples of the finest restaurants, clubs, and nighttime delights in Frankfurt. The city's dynamic nightlife scene ensures that there is something to suit every preference, whether you're looking for a gourmet dining experience, an energetic club, or a cozy bar to relax and unwind.

Frankfurt Itineraries Unveiling the Best of Frankfurt

Exploring the best of Frankfurt requires a well-planned itinerary that covers the city's cultural landmarks, historical sites, culinary delights, and vibrant neighborhoods. Here are seven days sample itineraries that unveil the best of Frankfurt:

7 days Itineraries Unveiling the Best of Frankfurt

Day 1: Explore the Historic Center

Start your day by visiting the Römerberg, the historic heart of Frankfurt. Admire the medieval buildings, including the famous Römer, the city hall.

Visit the Frankfurt Cathedral, a stunning Gothic structure with impressive views from its tower.

Explore the Museum Embankment, home to a variety of museums, including the Städel Museum, which houses an impressive collection of European art.

Enjoy a leisurely walk along the Main River, taking in the picturesque views and stopping at one of the riverfront cafes for a coffee or a snack.

In the evening, head to Sachsenhausen district, known for its traditional apple wine taverns. Sample the local apple wine and savor traditional German dishes.

Day 2: Modern Frankfurt and Skyline Views

Start your day at the Main Tower, the city's tallest building. Take the elevator to the observation deck for panoramic views of Frankfurt's skyline.

Visit the Palmengarten, a beautiful botanical garden featuring a variety of plant species from around the world.

Explore the Museumsufer, the museum district along the Main River. Visit the Museum of Modern Art (MMK) or the German Film Museum.

In the evening, dine at one of Frankfurt's modern restaurants, offering innovative cuisine and stylish ambiance.

Day 3: Day Trip to Heidelberg

Take a day trip to Heidelberg, a charming town located about an hour from Frankfurt. Explore the historic center and visit the famous Heidelberg Castle.

Take a stroll along the Philosopher's Walk, a scenic path that offers stunning views of the town and the Neckar River.

Enjoy a traditional German meal at one of the local restaurants, or indulge in some of the town's renowned pastries.

Day 4: Nature and Outdoor Activities

Head to the Taunus Mountains, located just outside of Frankfurt, for a day of outdoor adventures. Go hiking or biking along the numerous trails, or simply enjoy the tranquility of nature.

Visit the Hessenpark Open-Air Museum, an outdoor museum showcasing traditional half-timbered houses and rural life in the region.

Relax in one of the nearby spa towns, such as Bad Homburg or Wiesbaden, and indulge in a spa treatment or wellness experience.

Day 5: Rheingau Wine Region

Embark on a day trip to the Rheingau wine region, known for its picturesque vineyards and excellent wines. Take a scenic drive along the Rhine River and visit some of the charming wineries and wine estates.

Enjoy wine tastings, learn about the winemaking process, and take in the breathtaking views of the vineyards.

Explore the town of Rüdesheim and take a cable car ride to the Niederwald Monument for panoramic views of the Rhine Valley.

Day 6: Cultural Delights and Shopping

Visit the Goethe House, the birthplace of renowned German writer Johann Wolfgang von Goethe. Explore the museum and learn about Goethe's life and literary works.

Stroll along the Zeil, Frankfurt's main shopping street, lined with a variety of shops, boutiques, and department stores.

Explore the Kleinmarkthalle, a vibrant market hall where you can sample local specialties and purchase fresh produce, meats, and cheeses.

Day 7: Day Trip to the Black Forest

Take a day trip to the Black Forest, a scenic region known for its dense forests, charming villages, and traditional craftsmanship.

Visit the town of Triberg, famous for its cuckoo clocks and beautiful waterfalls.

Explore the scenic hiking trails or take a leisurely drive through the picturesque countryside.

Indulge in some local Black Forest cuisine, such as Black Forest cake or a hearty meal featuring regional specialties like Black Forest ham and game dishes.

Immerse yourself in the cultural heritage of the Black Forest by visiting open-air museums like the Vogtsbauernhof or the Schwarzwälder Freilichtmuseum. These museums showcase traditional Black Forest architecture and offer insights into the region's history and customs.

Take a scenic drive along the Schwarzwaldhochstraße (Black Forest High Road), a panoramic route that winds through the forested mountains, offering stunning vistas and picturesque villages along the way.

If you're interested in outdoor activities, the Black Forest offers numerous opportunities. Go hiking or cycling on the well-marked trails that traverse the region, or try your hand at winter sports like skiing or snowboarding during the snowy months.

Discover the enchanting charm of the Black Forest's spa towns, such as Baden-Baden or Bad Wildbad. Relax in the thermal baths, indulge in spa treatments, or take a leisurely stroll through the beautifully landscaped parks and gardens.

Don't miss the chance to taste the local Black Forest cherry liqueur, known as Schwarzwälder Kirsch. Visit a distillery or tavern to sample this famous regional specialty.

In the evening, return to Frankfurt and conclude your day with a delightful dinner at one of the city's renowned restaurants, where you can savor international cuisine or indulge in a traditional German feast.

These itineraries offer a comprehensive overview of the best that Frankfurt and its surrounding areas have to offer. Whether you're interested in exploring the city's historic center, immersing yourself in nature, or venturing out to nearby regions, you'll have a week filled with diverse experiences and unforgettable memories.

Transportation in Frankfurt Navigating the Scenic Routes

Frankfurt offers a well-connected transportation system that makes it easy to navigate the city and explore its scenic routes. Here's a detailed overview of transportation options in Frankfurt:

Public Transportation

Frankfurt has an extensive public transportation network, including buses, trams, and trains operated by Rhein-Main-Verkehrsverbund (RMV). The public transportation system provides convenient access to various parts of the city and its surrounding areas.

The U-Bahn (subway) and S-Bahn (commuter trains) are efficient modes of transportation, with frequent service and extensive coverage. They are ideal for traveling within the city and connecting to neighboring towns.

Trams and buses complement the rail network and offer additional flexibility in reaching specific destinations within Frankfurt.

Regional Trains

Frankfurt's main train station, Frankfurt Hauptbahnhof, is a major transportation hub and serves as a gateway to other cities in Germany and Europe. Regional trains connect Frankfurt to nearby towns, allowing you to easily explore the scenic routes and countryside.

The Rhein-Main-Verkehrsverbund (RMV) ticketing system covers regional train services, enabling you to purchase a single ticket for seamless travel across different modes of transportation.

Cycling

Frankfurt is a bike-friendly city with well-maintained cycling paths and bike rental services available. Renting a bike is a great way to explore the city's scenic routes and enjoy the picturesque landscapes.

The Main River promenade offers a popular cycling route, allowing you to pedal along the riverbanks and soak in the scenic beauty of the surroundings.

Bike-sharing programs, such as Call a Bike or Nextbike, provide convenient options for renting bikes on a short-term basis.

Scenic Routes and Day Trips

Exploring the scenic routes around Frankfurt is a must. Renting a car allows you to venture beyond the city limits and discover the picturesque countryside at your own pace.

The Taunus Mountains, located just outside Frankfurt, offer stunning landscapes and idyllic hiking trails. Renting a car or joining an organized tour enables you to access the mountainous regions and enjoy the scenic routes.

The Rhein River Valley, a UNESCO World Heritage site, is easily accessible from Frankfurt. Rent a car or take a guided tour to experience the charming towns, vineyards, and castles along the river.

Taxis and Ride-Sharing

Taxis are readily available in Frankfurt, and you can easily find them at designated taxi stands or hail them on the street.

Ride-sharing services like Uber are also operational in Frankfurt, providing convenient and flexible transportation options.

Parking

If you choose to drive in Frankfurt, be aware that parking in the city center can be challenging and expensive. Look for public parking garages or designated parking areas.

Ticketing and Fares

The RMV ticketing system covers all modes of public transportation in Frankfurt and the surrounding region. You can purchase single tickets, day passes, or multi-day passes depending on your travel needs. Make sure to validate your ticket before boarding public transportation.

With a reliable public transportation system, regional train connections, bike-friendly infrastructure, and the option to rent cars or join organized tours, navigating Frankfurt and its scenic routes is convenient and accessible. Enjoy exploring the city's stunning surroundings and immerse yourself in the beauty of the region.

Language

In Frankfurt, the predominant language spoken is German. As the largest city in the state of Hesse and a major economic hub in Germany, German is the official language used in government, business, and everyday interactions. However, due to its international nature and a large expatriate community, English is also commonly spoken, especially in tourist areas, hotels, restaurants, and businesses catering to international visitors. Here's some detailed information about language in Frankfurt:

German Language

Learning a few basic German phrases and greetings can greatly enhance your experience in Frankfurt. Locals appreciate the effort made to communicate in their native language.

Most signs, menus, and public announcements are in German. It is helpful to familiarize yourself with common phrases and words to navigate the city and understand important information.

If you encounter any language difficulties, don't hesitate to ask for assistance. Many Germans are proficient in English and will gladly help you.

English Language

English is widely understood in Frankfurt, particularly in areas with heavy tourist traffic and international businesses. Most hotel staff, restaurant servers, and shopkeepers can communicate in English.

Many tourist attractions, museums, and information centers provide English-language brochures, audio guides, and signage.

English-speaking expatriate communities and international organizations in Frankfurt contribute to the availability of English services and resources.

Language Services

Frankfurt has language schools and institutes that offer German language courses for foreigners. These programs cater to various proficiency levels and can help you learn or improve your German language skills.

Translators and interpreters are available in Frankfurt for official and business purposes. If you require professional language services, you can find translation agencies and freelance translators in the city.

Cultural Considerations

Germans generally appreciate when visitors attempt to speak German. Even basic greetings like "Guten Tag" (Good day) or "Danke" (Thank you) can go a long way in showing respect for the local culture.

Germans tend to be direct in their communication style, so don't be surprised if conversations are straightforward and to the point.

It's important to be mindful of cultural norms and etiquette while interacting with locals. Being polite and using appropriate greetings and phrases will help create a positive impression.

Greetings and Basic Phrases

Greetings:

Guten Morgen! (Good morning!)

Guten Tag! (Good day!)

Guten Abend! (Good evening!)

Hallo! (Hello!)

Grüß Gott! (A common greeting in southern Germany)

Introducing Yourself:

Mein Name ist... (My name is...)

Ich komme aus... (I'm from...)

Es freut mich, Sie kennenzulernen. (Nice to meet you)

Polite Expressions:

Bitte. (Please.)

Danke. (Thank you.)

Danke schön. (Thank you very much.)

Entschuldigung. (Excuse me.)

Entschuldigen Sie bitte. (Excuse me, please.)

Es tut mir leid. (I'm sorry.)

Basic Conversation Phrases:

Wie geht es Ihnen? (How are you?)

Mir geht es gut. (I'm doing well.)

Sprechen Sie Englisch? (Do you speak English?)

Ich spreche kein Deutsch. (I don't speak German.)

Können Sie das bitte wiederholen? (Can you please repeat that?)

Verstehen Sie mich? (Do you understand me?)

Ja. (Yes.)

Nein. (No.)

Ordering Food and Drinks:

Eine Tasse Kaffee, bitte. (A cup of coffee, please)

Ich möchte gerne... (I would like...)

Die Rechnung, bitte. (The bill, please.)

Prost! (Cheers!)

Asking for Directions:

Entschuldigen Sie, wo ist...? (Excuse me, where is...?)

Wie komme ich zum...? (How do I get to...?)

Ist es weit von hier? (Is it far from here?)

Links. (Left.)

Rechts. (Right.)

Geradeaus. (Straight ahead.)

Remember, making an effort to speak German, even if it's just a few basic phrases, is greatly appreciated by the locals. They will be more willing to assist you and it will enhance your overall experience in Frankfurt. Don't be afraid to ask for help or clarification if needed. Enjoy your time in Frankfurt!

Engaging in Conversation

Engaging in conversation with locals in Frankfurt can be a rewarding experience that allows you to connect with the city's culture and people. Here are some tips and phrases to help you engage in conversation while in Frankfurt:

Start with a Polite Greeting:

Greet people with a friendly "Guten Morgen" (Good morning), "Guten Tag" (Good day), or "Guten Abend" (Good evening) based on the time of day.

If you're meeting someone for the first time, a simple "Hallo" (Hello) or "Grüß Gott" (A common greeting in southern Germany) will suffice.

Show Interest and Ask Questions:

Germans appreciate genuine interest in their culture and city. Ask questions about local attractions, traditions, or current events.

Examples: "Wie gefällt Ihnen Frankfurt?" (How do you like Frankfurt?), "Was sind einige der besten Sehenswürdigkeiten hier?" (What are some of the best sights here?), or "Gibt es lokale Veranstaltungen oder Feste, die Sie empfehlen können?" (Are there any local events or festivals you can recommend?).

Practice Basic German Phrases:

Even if your German skills are limited, locals will appreciate your efforts to communicate in their language. Use simple phrases like "Entschuldigung" (Excuse me), "Bitte" (Please), and "Danke" (Thank you).

If you don't understand something, politely say "Können Sie das bitte wiederholen?" (Can you please repeat that?) Or "Ich verstehe nicht" (I don't understand).

Talk About Shared Interests:

If you find common interests or hobbies, it can be a great icebreaker. For example, if you're at an art gallery strikes up a conversation about the artwork ask for recommendations on local cultural events.

Engage in conversations about sports, music, food, or any topics you have knowledge or curiosity about.

Be Respectful of Personal Space and Cultural Differences:

Germans value personal space and may prefer a more formal approach, especially in initial interactions. Avoid invading personal space and maintain an appropriate distance.

Be mindful of cultural differences and avoid controversial topics or sensitive issues unless the other person brings them up.

Listen and Be Engaged:

Active listening is important in any conversation. Show genuine interest, maintain eye contact, and nod to indicate that you are engaged.

Use appropriate non-verbal cues to show understanding and agreement.

Enjoy Local Cuisine and Beverages:

Frankfurt offers a vibrant food and drink scene. Engage in conversations about local cuisine, wines, or beers. Ask for recommendations on local dishes or specialties.

Remember, building rapport takes time, so don't be discouraged if conversations start off a bit reserved. Be patient, open-minded, and respectful, and you'll have a great time engaging in conversations with locals in Frankfurt.

Ordering Food and Drinks

Ordering food and drinks in Frankfurt can be an enjoyable experience, allowing you to savor the city's culinary delights. Here's a guide to help you navigate the process:

Choosing a Restaurant:

Frankfurt offers a wide range of dining options, from traditional German cuisine to international flavors. Research local restaurants, read reviews, and consider the type of food you're interested in.

Popular areas for dining in Frankfurt include Sachsenhausen, the city center, and the Bahnhofsviertel district.

Greeting and Seating:

Upon entering a restaurant, wait to be seated or ask the host/hostess, "Haben Sie einen Tisch frei?" (Do you have a table available?)

If the seating is open, you can choose a table and say, "Wir möchten gerne hier sitzen" (We would like to sit here).

Ordering Food:

Once seated, the waiter/waitress will usually provide you with menus. Take your time to browse the selections.

When ready to order, politely call the waiter/waitress by saying, "Entschuldigung" (Excuse me) or "Bitte" (Please) to get their attention.

Start by saying, "Ich hätte gerne..." (I would like...) followed by the dish or item you want to order. For example, "Ich hätte gerne die Frankfurter Grüne Soße" (I would like the Frankfurt green sauce).

Special Dietary Requests:

If you have any dietary restrictions or preferences, such as being vegetarian, vegan, or having food allergies, inform the waiter/waitress by saying, "Ich bin Vegetarier/Veganer. Haben Sie vegetarische/vegane Optionen?" (I am a vegetarian/vegan. Do you have vegetarian/vegan options?)

Ordering Drinks:

To order drinks, you can say, "Ich möchte bitte ein Bier/Wein/Wasser" (I would like a beer/wine/water).

If you're interested in trying a local specialty, ask for recommendations such as "Welchen Wein empfehlen Sie?" (Which wine do you recommend?)

Asking for the Bill:

When you're ready to pay, say, "Die Rechnung, bitte" (The bill, please).

In some restaurants, the bill may be brought to you automatically once you finish your meal.

Tipping:

In Frankfurt, it is customary to leave a tip. A common practice is to round up the bill or leave around 10% of the total amount as a tip. You can give the tip directly to the waiter/waitress when paying the bill.

Common Phrases:

"Ein Tisch für zwei, bitte" (A table for two, please)

"Können Sie die Speisekarte bitte erklären?" (Can you please explain the menu?)

"Haben Sie Empfehlungen?" (Do you have any recommendations?)

"Noch eine Minute, bitte" (One more minute, please)

"Könnten Sie bitte das Wasser auffüllen?" (Could you please refill the water?)

Remember to be polite and patient during the ordering process. The staffs in Frankfurt's restaurants are generally friendly and accommodating. Enjoy the delicious food and drinks that Frankfurt has to offer!

Exploring the Markets

xploring the markets in Frankfurt is a delightful experience that allows you to immerse yourself in the city's vibrant atmosphere, discover local products, and engage with the community. Here are some of the most popular markets worth exploring:

Kleinmarkthalle:

Located in the city center, Kleinmarkthalle is a bustling indoor market that offers a wide array of fresh produce, meats, cheeses, baked goods, and international delicacies.

Stroll through the market, interact with the friendly vendors, and sample the various food offerings. Don't miss the opportunity to try traditional Frankfurt specialties like Grüne Soße (green sauce) and Handkäse mit Musik (marinated cheese).

Frankfurter Wochenmarkt:

Held every Wednesday and Saturday at the Konstablerwache Square, Frankfurter Wochenmarkt is one of the largest outdoor markets in Frankfurt.

Browse through the stalls filled with seasonal fruits, vegetables, flowers, herbs, and other regional products. You'll also find a variety of food stands offering snacks and refreshments.

Flohmarkt am Mainufer:

The Flohmarkt am Mainufer is a popular flea market held along the banks of the Main River on Saturdays. It's a treasure trove of antiques, vintage items, clothing, accessories, and unique collectibles.

Spend a leisurely morning or afternoon exploring the stalls, bargaining with the vendors, and finding one-of-a-kind items to take home as souvenirs.

Schillermarkt:

The Schillermarkt is a charming neighborhood market located in the Nordend district. It takes place every Thursday and Saturday and offers a mix of fresh produce, artisanal food products, and handmade crafts.

Enjoy the relaxed atmosphere, chat with local vendors, and savor the flavors of regional products. The market is particularly known for its selection of organic and sustainable goods.

Berger Markt:

Berger Markt is another vibrant neighborhood market situated in the

Bornheim district. It takes place every Wednesday and Saturday, attracting locals and visitors alike.

Discover a diverse range of products, including fresh fruits and vegetables, meats, cheeses, flowers, clothing, and household items. Take your time to explore the stalls and soak up the lively atmosphere.

Christmas Markets:

During the holiday season, Frankfurt is renowned for its enchanting Christmas markets. The most famous one is the Frankfurt Christmas Market, held in the city center. It features festive decorations, sparkling lights, handmade crafts, delicious food, and warm Glühwein (mulled wine).

Explore the various stalls, enjoy traditional Christmas treats like Lebkuchen (gingerbread) and Bratwurst, and indulge in the joyful atmosphere of the season.

While exploring the markets, remember to bring cash as some vendors may not accept cards. Embrace the opportunity to interact with the vendors, practice your German language skills, and experience the local culture. The markets in Frankfurt provide a unique glimpse into the city's culinary traditions, craftsmanship, and community spirit.

Getting Around

Getting around in Frankfurt is relatively easy, thanks to its efficient and well-connected transportation system. Here are some key phrases and information to help you navigate the city:

Public Transportation:

"Wo ist die nächste U-Bahn?" - Where is the nearest subway?

"Wie komme ich zur S-Bahn-Station?" - How do I get to the S-Bahn station?

"Wann fährt der nächste Bus ab?" - When does the next bus depart?

"Ein Ticket nach [destination], bitte." - One ticket to [destination], please.

"Welche Linie fährt zum Hauptbahnhof?" - Which line goes to the main train station?

"Wo kann ich ein Ticket kaufen?" - Where can I buy a ticket?

Taxis and Ride-Sharing:

"Könnten Sie mich zum [destination] bringen?" - Could you take me to [destination]?

"Wie viel kostet eine Fahrt zum Flughafen?" - How much does a ride to the airport cost?

"Können Sie bitte den Taximeter einschalten?" - Could you please turn on the taxi meter?

"Ich möchte gerne einen Uber bestellen." - I would like to order an Uber.

Asking for Directions:

"Entschuldigung, können Sie mir bitte den Weg zur [destination] zeigen?" - Excuse me, could you please show me the way to [destination]?

"Wie komme ich zum nächsten Park?" - How do I get to the nearest park?

"Ist das hier der richtige Weg zum Museum?" - Is this the right way to the museum?

Renting a Bicycle:

"Wo kann ich ein Fahrrad mieten?" - Where can I rent a bicycle?

"Wie viel kostet die Tagesmiete?" - How much does it cost for a full day rental?

"Gibt es Radwege in der Stadt?" - Are there bike lanes in the city?

"Könnten Sie mir bitte eine Karte mit den Fahrradwegen geben?" - Could you please give me a map of the bike paths?

Walking:

"Wie weit ist es bis zum Dom?" - How far is it to the cathedral?

"Gibt es einen Fußgängerweg zur Altstadt?" - Is there a pedestrian path to the old town?

"Können Sie mir bitte den Weg zum Park zeigen?" - Could you please show me the way to the park?

Other Useful Phrases:

"Entschuldigung" - Excuse me.

"Danke" - Thank you.

"Bitte" - Please/you're welcome.

"Sprechen Sie Englisch?" - Do you speak English?

"Ich verstehe nicht" - I don't understand.

"Können Sie das bitte wiederholen?" - Could you please repeat that?

"Hilfe" - Help!

Remember to speak clearly and politely when asking for directions or using public transportation. Frankfurt has a diverse population, and many locals are familiar with English. However, learning a few basic phrases in German will always come in handy and can enhance your overall experience in navigating the city.

Traditional Frankfurt Sayings and Proverbs

Traditional Frankfurt sayings and proverbs reflect the unique culture, dialect, and humor of the city. Here are some popular ones:

"Ebbelwoi un Handkäs, mehr brauchd'r net zu wisse." (Cider and marinated cheese, that's all you need to know.)

This saying highlights two iconic Frankfurt specialties, Ebbelwoi (apple wine) and Handkäs (marinated cheese). It implies that life's simple pleasures are often the best.

"Es geht net um die Worscht, sondern um die Worschtsemmel." (It's not about the sausage, but about the bread roll.

This saying emphasizes that it's the little details that matter. It's not just about the main event, but also the accompanying elements that complete the experience.

"Es geht drunner und drüber wie uffm Römerberch." (It's chaotic like on Römerberg.)

Römerberg is the historic square in Frankfurt's old town known for its lively atmosphere. This saying implies a situation of chaos or disorder.

"Wie die Frankfurter gudd Ess und Trink, so babbelt er." (As a Frankfurter eats and drinks, so he talks.)

This saying suggests that the people of Frankfurt love good food and drink, and they are equally expressive and talkative.

"Wer nichts wird, wird Wirt in Sachsenhausen." (Whoever amounts to nothing becomes an innkeeper in Sachsenhausen.)

Sachsenhausen is a district in Frankfurt known for its vibrant nightlife and numerous traditional taverns. This saying humorously suggests that those who don't succeed in other ventures end up becoming innkeepers there.

"Des is wie am Dom ebbes los." (It's busy like at the cathedral.)

Referring to the bustling Frankfurt Cathedral (Dom), this saying signifies a busy and lively situation.

"Scho wo's Fähnche weht, wird e'Fescht gefiert." (Where the flag is flying, a festival is celebrated.)

This saying highlights the festive spirit of Frankfurt and its tradition of celebrating various occasions and events.

"Frankfurter sind auch net grad weltverlore." (Frankfurters are not exactly naive.)

This saying suggests that the people of Frankfurt are astute and savvy, not easily fooled or naive.

These traditional sayings and proverbs provide insight into the humor, customs, and character of Frankfurt. They are part of the local identity and offer a glimpse into the unique linguistic and cultural aspects of the city.

Frankfurt Literature and Poetry

Frankfurt has a rich literary tradition and has been home to many renowned writers and poets. Here is an overview of Frankfurt's literature and poetry scene:

Johann Wolfgang von Goethe:

Frankfurt's most famous literary figure is Johann Wolfgang von Goethe (1749-1832), one of Germany's greatest writers. Goethe was born in Frankfurt and spent his early years in the city. His works, such as "Faust" and "The Sorrows of Young Werther," have had a profound impact on German literature and continue to be celebrated worldwide.

The Frankfurt Book Fair:

Frankfurt is also known for hosting the Frankfurt Book Fair, one of the largest and most important book fairs in the world. It takes place annually and attracts publishers, authors, literary agents, and book lovers from around the globe. The fair showcases a vast array of books and serves as a platform for networking and business opportunities in the publishing industry.

The German National Library:

The German National Library, located in Frankfurt, is a significant institution for literature and research. It serves as the central archival and bibliographic resource for German-language publications. It houses an extensive collection of books, manuscripts, and other literary works, making it an essential destination for scholars and researchers.

Literary Events and Festivals:

Frankfurt hosts various literary events and festivals throughout the year, celebrating literature in its diverse forms. The Literaturhaus Frankfurt, a cultural institution dedicated to promoting literature, organizes readings, discussions, and exhibitions. The

Open Books Festival, associated with the Frankfurt Book Fair, features readings by national and international authors.

Poets and Writers:

Besides Goethe, Frankfurt has been home to other notable poets and writers. Friedrich Stoltze (1816-1891), a local poet and journalist, played a significant role in preserving the Frankfurt dialect and cultural heritage through his satirical works. Heinrich Hoffmann (1809-1894), the author of the well-known children's book "Der Struwwelpeter," was also born in Frankfurt.

Literary Landmarks:

Frankfurt boasts several literary landmarks that offer insights into its literary heritage. The Goethe House and Goethe Museum provide a glimpse into the life and works of Johann Wolfgang von Goethe. The Schirn Kunsthalle Frankfurt, an art museum, often hosts exhibitions and events exploring the intersection of art and literature.

Literary Cafés and Bookstores:

Frankfurt offers a vibrant literary café and bookstore scene. Cafés like Morgenstund and Proust are known for their cozy atmosphere and literary events. Bookstores such as Hugendubel, Dussmann das KulturKaufhaus, and Buchhandlung Schutt attract bibliophiles with their extensive selections of books, including works by local and international authors.

Frankfurt's literary and poetic legacy is a testament to its cultural significance. The city continues to nurture and celebrate literature through its institutions, festivals, and vibrant literary community, making it an inspiring destination for book lovers and literary enthusiasts alike.

Cultural Etiquette

When visiting Frankfurt, it's helpful to be aware of the cultural etiquette to ensure respectful and positive interactions with locals. Here are some key points to keep in mind:

Greetings and Politeness:

When meeting someone for the first time, it is customary to offer a handshake and maintain eye contact.

Address people using their titles and last names unless they invite you to use their first name.

Politeness and courtesy are highly valued, so saying "please" (bitte) and "thank you" (danke) are important in daily interactions.

Punctuality and Reliability:

Germans, including those in Frankfurt, place great importance on punctuality and being reliable. It's considered respectful to arrive on time for appointments, meetings, and social gatherings.

Personal Space and Privacy:

Germans generally value their personal space, so it's important to respect a comfortable distance when interacting with others. Avoid standing too close or touching someone unless you have a close relationship.

Privacy is also highly respected, so it's advisable to avoid prying into personal matters unless the other person voluntarily shares.

Respect for Rules and Order:

Frankfurt is known for its efficient and organized systems. It is important to follow rules, such as waiting for the traffic signal to cross the road and adhering to public transportation etiquette.

Germans value cleanliness, so littering or leaving a mess in public spaces is considered disrespectful.

Dining Etiquette:

When dining in a restaurant, it's customary to wait to be seated rather than choosing your own table.

Maintain proper table manners, including using utensils appropriately and keeping your elbows off the table.

It is polite to say "Guten Appetit" (Enjoy your meal) before starting to eat and to finish everything on your plate as wasting food is generally frowned upon.

Quiet and Considerate Behavior:

Frankfurt, like many German cities, appreciates quiet and peaceful environments. Speaking loudly or causing disturbances in public places, such as libraries or public transportation, is considered impolite.

It is also important to turn off or silence your mobile phone in theaters, museums, and other quiet spaces.

Dress Code:

Frankfurt has a diverse range of styles, but generally, people dress neatly and conservatively. Business attire is expected in formal settings, while casual and smart-casual attire is suitable for most other occasions.

By observing these cultural etiquettes in Frankfurt, you will show respect for local customs and contribute to a positive and harmonious experience during your visit.

Language Learning Resources

Frankfurt offers a range of language learning resources for those interested in studying German or other languages. Here are some options available:

Language Schools:

Frankfurt is home to several language schools that offer courses for different proficiency levels. These schools provide structured language programs taught by experienced instructors. Examples include Goethe-Institut Frankfurt, Berlitz Frankfurt, and Inlingua Frankfurt.

Volkshochschule (Adult Education Centers):

The Volkshochschule in Frankfurt is a public institution that offers language courses for adults. They provide a wide range of language programs, including German courses for foreigners, conversation classes, and specialized language workshops. These courses are usually affordable and cater to different schedules and levels of proficiency.

University Language Centers:

Frankfurt is home to several universities with language centers that offer language courses to students and the general public. These centers provide comprehensive language programs, including German as a foreign language, as well as courses in other languages.

Language Exchange Groups:

Language exchange groups in Frankfurt offer a platform for language learners to practice their skills with native speakers. These groups typically organize regular meetups where participants can engage in conversation exchanges and cultural activities. Examples include Tandem Frankfurt and Meetup language exchange groups.

Online Language Learning Platforms:

There are numerous online language learning platforms that provide interactive lessons, exercises, and language resources. Platforms like Duolingo, Babbel, and Rosetta Stone offer German courses designed for self-paced learning. These platforms often include audio recordings, vocabulary exercises, and interactive lessons.

Libraries:

Frankfurt's public libraries have a collection of language learning materials, including books, CDs, and online resources. The

Frankfurt City Library (Stadtbibliothek Frankfurt) and University Libraries offer language learning materials that can be borrowed for self-study.

Language Meetups and Language Cafés:

Language meetups and language cafés in Frankfurt provide opportunities for language learners to practice their skills in a relaxed and informal setting. These events often bring together language enthusiasts from different backgrounds and offer a supportive environment for language exchange.

Language Apps and Online Resources:

There are various language learning apps and online resources that can be accessed from anywhere. Apps like Memrise, Lingoda, and FluentU provide language courses, vocabulary practice, and interactive exercises. Online resources such as Deutsche Welle and BBC Languages offer free language lessons and multimedia content.

Whether you prefer classroom-based learning, one-on-one instruction, online platforms, or language exchange opportunities, Frankfurt has a range of resources to support your language learning journey. Choose the option that best suits your needs and learning style to enhance your language skills while immersing yourself in the vibrant multicultural environment of Frankfurt.

Conclusion

the book "Frankfurt Travel Guide: The Ultimate Guide to Unveiling Frankfurt's Ancient History, Art, Culture, Culinary Delights, and Breathtaking Outdoor Activities" serves as an invaluable resource for anyone seeking to explore the vibrant and captivating city of Frankfurt. Throughout its pages, readers are treated to a comprehensive and immersive journey, uncovering the hidden gems and rich tapestry of this remarkable destination.

By delving into Frankfurt's ancient history, the book illuminates the city's roots, offering a deeper understanding of its evolution and significance. From its medieval origins to its rise as a financial powerhouse, the guide paints a vivid picture of Frankfurt's past, allowing visitors to appreciate the layers of heritage that shape its present-day allure.

Art and culture enthusiasts will find themselves enthralled as they discover Frankfurt's thriving arts scene. From world-class museums housing masterpieces to cutting-edge galleries showcasing contemporary works, the guide showcases the city's artistic prowess in all its splendor. Whether it's exploring the iconic Städel Museum or attending captivating performances at the Frankfurt Opera House, the book directs readers to the cultural landmarks that should not be missed.

Moreover, the culinary delights of Frankfurt are laid bare, enticing readers with a tantalizing array of flavors and tastes. From the traditional Apfelwein taverns serving hearty local cuisine to the innovative gourmet restaurants pushing culinary boundaries, the guide ensures that gastronomic adventurers are well-equipped to savor every delectable bite Frankfurt has to offer.

For those seeking outdoor adventures, the book reveals the city's breathtaking landscapes and recreational opportunities. From strolling along the scenic banks of the Main River to exploring the lush greenery of the nearby Taunus Mountains, readers are guided towards outdoor activities that allow them to recharge and reconnect with nature.

Ultimately, "Frankfurt Travel Guide" is more than just a collection of recommendations; it is a passport to immersing oneself in the authentic spirit of this remarkable city. With its wealth of information, insider tips, and captivating storytelling, the guide empowers travelers to create unforgettable memories, unlocking the hidden wonders that make Frankfurt a truly exceptional destination. Whether it's a first-time visit or a return trip, this comprehensive guide is an indispensable companion for anyone seeking to unravel the secrets and embrace the wonders of Frankfurt.

Made in United States
Troutdale, OR
10/19/2024

23903552R00130